# ENDOR

"Thank you for bringing the _ paradigm in relief and development work to the forefront: *Kingdom Outposts* is a timely and incredibly important work for our churches and Christ-centered development organizations. While a variety of theories exist on international development, few are from a biblical perspective. With lucid writing, *Kingdom Outposts* will be invaluable to Christian leaders, churches, and the everyday disciple of Jesus interested in making a difference. Thank you for writing it!"
—Peter Greer, President and CEO, HOPE International and author of *The Spiritual Danger of Doing Good*

"Dru Dodson has made an important contribution to the thinking of how churches collaborate for training and development in very challenging contexts. Dru brings decades of credibility as a local church pastor, church planter, and missiologist. He is a delightful leader who finds great joy in seeing the kingdom grow in the hardest places."
—Dr. Mac Pier, CEO and Founder, The New York City Leadership Center

"On this, the fourth anniversary of the worst urban natural disaster in human history—the earthquake that shook Port-au-Prince on January 12, 2010—Dru Dodson draws our attention to a fresh theology for what relief and development might look like. His learnings in Haïti shape the book. Our mutual love for missional theology and action in that country drew me to the text. This is a fine contribution to the growing literature on what needs to change in how agencies and local churches think about their ministries."
—Dr. Glenn Smith, Executive Director, Christian Direction, Montréal; Professor of Contextual Theologies, Université Chrétienne du Nord d'Haïti; Academic Dean, Institut de théologie pour la Francophonie (Université Laval) Montréal

"Recommendations for relief and development that are truly based in the work of apostolic teams and church networks are uncommon. *Kingdom Outposts* emphasizes that the biblical solution includes long-term support for needs beyond the urgent physical crisis. The way of Christ and his apostles calls for priority to be given to establishment of believers' faith and strengthening of churches in a manner that prioritizes development of godly leaders and their engagement in culture. Hence, we are glad to partner in leadership development using BILD International resources and degree programs of its Antioch School of Church Planting and Leadership Development."

—Dr. Steve Kemp, Academic Dean, The Antioch School of Church Planting and Leadership Development

"We at Go2 Network are blessed to have a working apostolic leader like Dr. Dru Dodson on our team! You will find his insights and understandings on relief and development an alternative to so much happening today in this area. May the challenge you receive here spur you on to many good works for the glory of our Lord Jesus!"

—Dr. Tim Boal, President, The Go2 Network

"This book by Dru Dodson is truly a labor of love and a unique gift to all of us engaged in completing the mission of Jesus Christ! Dru reminds us that abundant life for the poor is an integral part of Jesus' good news of the Kingdom, and pointedly documents the false dichotomy created between evangelism and relief and development efforts. Through his first-hand experience of leading Lake Valley Community Church in a partnership in Haiti, he presents an inspiring vision of shalom, through the local church and business people building community. This is a must read!"

—Doug Seebeck, President, Partners Worldwide

# Dru Dodson

# KINGDOM OUTPOSTS

## A Fresh Theology of Relief and Development

*Printed in the United States of America*

For Jo Helen, my love and partner. The fruit of this thesis will likely result in yet another season of pioneering start-ups. I look forward to doing it together with you!

In an important sense, development
is a religious category...
Ultimately, it represents a secularization
of biblical eschatology...
Its success as a new gospel has been enormous.
– *Peter Berger, Pyramids of Sacrifice*

[Biblical literature speaks] obliquely at times
but never abstractly of the situations and
concerns of ordinary people—that is, of people
who are not rich and who have to eat.
– *Ellen F. Davis, Scripture, Culture, and Agriculture*

# CONTENTS

# LIST OF FIGURES

# ACKNOWLEDGMENTS

Thank you to the elders and people of Lake Valley Community Church, Hot Springs, Arkansas. Your support to begin and finish this effort (!) has been invaluable. I could not have done it without you.

Thank you also to Jeff Reed and the Biblical Institute of Leadership Development. I've learned so much from your pioneering work and groundbreaking resources. Your whole church-based team and their sacrificial, dedicated work has been an example to me and to my church.

Finally, many thanks to Dr. Tim Boal for inviting me to help him with the Go2 Network! Your heart and vision for the American church motivates those of us who know you. I love startups, and I've loved working with you on Go2. The Go2 Network is a network of churches, pastors, theologians, and missionaries who are experienced in church planting, leadership development, and church renewal. We are seeking to demonstrate the beauty and believability of Jesus and his message to a changing American society. To that end, we engage in fresh theological dialogue to find, equip, and help release marketplace people into Jesus' mission.

# ABSTRACT

Relief and development (R&D) is best understood as a forgotten part of Jesus' gospel of the kingdom. A storied, church-based, biblical theology of R&D traces the themes of God, his people, and his land through the Scriptures. The thesis is developed that the kingdom of God advances over the earth through the apostolic establishment of new kingdom communities or outposts, which function according to a kingdom economics. These Kingdom Outposts are the locus of R&D done well.

The island nation of Haiti suffers extreme poverty, despite decades of evangelism and conventional R&D. This thesis explores an R&D project in Haiti in light of a theology of Kingdom Outposts.

# CHAPTER ONE

# THE PROBLEM AND ITS SETTING

The needs of the poor and oppressed in our world are overwhelming. One billion people are trapped in extreme poverty, trying to survive on less than $1.25 a day. Bright spots like India and China have raised the standard of living for millions, but billions are falling behind:

> The countries at the bottom coexist with the twenty-first century, but their reality is the fourteenth century: civil war, plague, ignorance. They are concentrated in Africa and Central Asia, with a scattering elsewhere... We must learn to turn the familiar numbers upside down: a total of five billion people who are already prosperous, or at least on track to be so, and one billion who are stuck at the bottom. (Collier 2007, 3)

There have been success stories, such as the eradication of polio. However, preventable diseases like malaria and diarrhea continue to kill millions of children and adults:

> Eight hundred and forty million people in the world don't have enough to eat. Ten million children die every year from easily preventable diseases. AIDS is killing three million people a year and is still spreading. One billion people in

the world lack access to clean water; two billion lack access to sanitation. One billion adults are illiterate. About a quarter of the children in the poor countries do not finish primary school... This poverty in the Rest justifiably moves many people in the West. (Easterly 2006, 7)

The statistics—and the reality they depict—can be overwhelming:

There are people who literally struggle to survive *every day of their lives*. The extent of this global poverty is staggering. As of July 2007, there were approximately 6.6 billion people living on earth. Approximately four billion live on less than $4 per day, nearly all of whom live in developing countries. (Greer and Smith 2009, 29)

While global efforts are making progress, recent statistics from the World Bank indicate that in 2010 some 1.2 billion people were still living on less than $1.25 per day:

We have made remarkable progress in reducing the number of people living under $1.25 a day in the developing world, but the fact that there are still 1.2 billion people in extreme poverty is a stain on our collective conscience. (World Bank president Jim Yong Kim, quoted in an April 17, 2013, World Bank press release)

In response to pervasive poverty, a massive aid or "relief and development" industry has arisen since World War II (see Moyo 2009, 10–28, for a history of the rise of this industry). I'll be using the terms *aid* and *relief and development* interchangeably. Relief and development

(R&D) can mean different things to different people. This thesis uses the phrase to refer firstly to emergency aid given to those affected by natural disasters, oppressive governments, economic collapse, and war. This is the "relief." The follow-up efforts to help these people rebuild their lives, economies, and societies are referred to as "development" (Greer and Smith 2009, 56). The usual assumption is that development should follow the lines of democratic, free-market capitalism (Berger 1976, 7–15). This assumption will be questioned in this thesis.

One approach to R&D is variously characterized as liberation theology, socialism, or Marxism. This point of view sees Western attempts at R&D as a thinly veiled effort to continue oppressing the poor. The literature of this tradition asserts that Western aid efforts actually prolong the problem of poverty—a problem that will only be cured by the rise (economically and militarily) of the poor and the (likely violent) overthrow of the rich (see Aristide 1990; Gutiérrez 1988; Petrella 2004). This approach represents a powerful paradigm and needs its own critique and correction by the gospel. However, it is beyond the scope of this project. (See Christian 1999, 47–49, for a brief survey.)

There are parallel R&D industries—an evangelical version and a secular or marketplace version. They sometimes cooperate but for the most part operate apart from each other. Evangelical R&D efforts are extensive, often comprised of short-term mission trips, construction projects, orphanages and schools, child sponsorship, clean water projects, business-as-mission initiatives, microfinance, and thousands of other permutations. For instance,

> There were 120,000 [short-term missionaries] in 1989, 450,000 in 1998, 1,000,000 in 2003, and 2,200,000 in 2006. The numbers reflect a tsunami of epic proportions, a tidal wave of American short-term "missionaries" flooding the world. The cost? Americans spent $1,600,000,000 on short-term missions (STMs) in 2006 alone. (Corbett and Fikkert 2009, 161)

The marketplace industry is even bigger, composed of both nongovernmental organizations (NGOs) and huge government initiatives like the United States Agency for International Development (USAID). Billions of dollars are raised or taxed to fund these efforts (Easterly 2006, 182–183). Hundreds of thousands of volunteers, donors, staff, consultants, development professionals, and bureaucrats are engaged in these R&D efforts. Thousands of for-profit businesses act as suppliers and contractors for NGO and government aid agencies. It is a huge industry. In addition to USAID, major organizations include the International Monetary Fund, the World Bank, the Food and Agriculture Association, the International Fund for Agricultural Development, the United Nations Development Program, the World Food Program, and the World Health Organization (Easterly 2006, 25; Sachs 2005, 286).

In recent years, a good deal of literature has been published critiquing the impact of these massive, well-intentioned efforts. Some of this literature will be reviewed in chapter three. Rampant corruption, particularly on the part of the governments of poor countries, dependency, and colonialism continue to be major problems (Easterly 2006, 112–121). While serving on a Rotary International delegation to Bulawayo, Zimbabwe for a well-drilling project, I was told by some Zimbabweans that the best thing that could happen for Africa would be for "all the NGOs to leave... now!" They were concerned about dependency. Much of the evangelical and secular literature analyzing R&D is overwhelmingly negative about current efforts to alleviate poverty. Note, for example, economist Dambisa Moyo's assessment:

> But has more than US$1 trillion in development assistance over the last several decades made African people better off? No. In fact, across the globe the recipients of this aid are worse off; much worse off. Aid has helped make the poor poorer, and growth slower. Yet aid remains a centrepiece of today's development policy and one of the biggest ideas of our time.
>
> The notion that aid can alleviate systemic poverty, and has done so, is a myth. Millions in Africa are poorer today because of aid; misery and poverty have not ended but have increased. Aid has been, and continues to be, an unmitigated political, economic, and humanitarian disaster for most parts of the developing world. (Moyo 2009, xix)

While Moyo is concerned about large governmental programs and their unintended consequences, Corbett and Fikkert are concerned about the unintended consequences of evangelical R&D efforts:

> By definition, short-term missions have only a short time in which to "show a profit," to achieve pre-defined goals. This can accentuate our American idols of speed, quantification, compartmentalization, money, achievement, and success. Projects become more important than people. The wells dug. Fifty people converted. Got to give the church back home a good report. Got to prove the time and expense was well worth it. To get the job done (on our time scale), imported technology becomes more important than contextualized methods. Individual drive becomes more important than respect for elders, for old courtesies, for taking time. We end up dancing like elephants. We dance hard, and we have big feet. (Miriam Adeney, quoted in Corbett and Fikkert 2009, 168)

The last ten years have seen a surge in the variety of evangelical responses to poverty. The whole business-as-mission (BAM) movement has sprung up in that time. Some authors are questioning the validity of short-term mission trips and offering alternatives (see Corbett and Fikkert, 2009). Job creation has become a viable mission effort. Evangelical microfinance organizations have been started. Christians have begun realizing the long-term value of training and business education. However, many of these newer movements in evangelicalism have co-opted the "kingdom" label to brand almost any effort to bring peace, justice, opportunity, and freedom to the poor and oppressed. And as we will see, almost all have unhooked the church from the kingdom and have bypassed or ignored local churches—both in the United States and abroad—in their "kingdom" solutions.

Conservative US Christianity continues to struggle with a false dichotomy of "evangelism and the gospel" versus "social action, justice, and mercy." Reams of literature are available proclaiming the priority of evangelism, or the priority of relief efforts in Jesus' name, or mercy and justice projects as "pre-evangelism." Much of the literature equates "mission" and "missionary" activity with "evangelism"—that is, personal conversion. A helpful example of this conversation can be found in Deyoung and Gilbert:

> Before we go any farther down the missional-corrective road, though, perhaps it would be helpful to make clear at the outset what we do and do not want to accomplish with this book.
>
> We do *not* want:
>
> - Christians to be indifferent toward the suffering around them and around the world.
> - Christians to think evangelism is the only thing in life that really counts.
> - Christians who risk their lives and sacrifice for the poor and disadvantaged to think their work is in any way suspect or is praise-worthy only if it results in conversions. (Deyoung and Gilbert 2011, 22)

Other voices call for identification with the poor, claiming that God has a "preferential option" for the poor, and understand our mission to be one of poverty alleviation, period. In the United States we have, of course, a long-standing fundamentalist-liberal divide over evangelism versus the "social gospel," a false dichotomy on which progress has certainly been made, though the tension is perhaps not yet resolved for everyone. (See Myers 2011 and Christian 1999 for good surveys of this discussion and literature.)

Bryant Myers, professor of transformational development at Fuller Theological Seminary, observes the following:

> Among evangelicals today the issue of social action versus evangelism is largely a historical footnote...
>
> This is all well and good, but it is important to say what has not happened in evangelical thinking about development. No case studies have been published in the last ten years. There are very few evaluations that are genuinely holistic...
>
> ...There is very little new theological reflection. We seem to be resting on the theological work done in the 1980s... We are not even all that significantly involved in the religion and development conversation that has changed so dramatically in the last ten years.
>
> There has been little fresh thinking on development ecclesiology. *Yet the question of the relationship between the Christian relief and development agency and local churches remains both unclear and problematic... Are churches mini-development agencies, members*

*of civil society, or something else altogether?*
(Myers 2011, 49, emphasis added)

## Kingdom Outposts

I am writing from the conviction that churches are "something else altogether," when understood in a kingdom framework as "Kingdom Outposts." Kingdom Outposts are Christian communities that have been fully established in the apostolic teaching and household order of Christ and his apostles. The apostles, having been trained and commissioned by Jesus himself and empowered by the promised Holy Spirit, were able to spread the gospel of the kingdom across the Roman Empire by planting and strengthening new communities. These new communities were intended to be local "demonstration projects" of the kingdom. That is, the life of each of these local communities was to be rooted in God's mission to redeem humanity along with all creation, and doing so in his way and in his image. "Your kingdom come, your will be done on earth as it is in heaven" (Matthew 6:10).

Put another way, these local communities were meant to be outposts of an encroaching civilization—namely, an encroaching civilization of God, living in *shalom* as God has always intended for humans and the earth. This encroaching, invading civilization—the kingdom of God—is distinctive from all other cultures and civilizations. Like yeast in dough or a seed in good soil, it takes root in its host culture and spreads its presence and influence until it has thoroughly transformed its host culture in accordance with God's vision. The seed that is planted does not consist solely of the verbal proclamation of the gospel; nor is it merely a converted individual. The seeds are newly established communities of kingdom culture, Kingdom Outposts.

Kingdom Outposts are communities of salvation. Because they have been established in the teaching of Christ and his apostles, they understand salvation as concerning more than the afterlife. Our presence with the Lord Jesus after our death is a precious promise and is indeed part of our salvation (see Philippians 1:23). There is, however, the after-afterlife as well—that is, the resurrection and the new heavens and new earth when we will once again be embodied and living in *shalom* as our Creator intended (see 1 Corinthians 15 and Revelation 21–22). This is the final goal of humanity. There is also a before-afterlife salvation, which is especially important to this thesis project.

A before-afterlife salvation involves many of the same goals for a community as contemporary R&D efforts. In fact, as will be noted in this thesis, contemporary R&D literature often articulates a secularized version of biblical expectation and eschatology. A Kingdom Outpost in particular has been established in the economic teaching of Christ and his apostles, a teaching that itself was rooted in the economics of the Torah, the Prophets and the Writings. So these Kingdom Outposts not only demonstrate a distinctive sexual morality, for instance, or distinctive practices like the Lord's Supper and baptism, *but they also demonstrate a distinctive economics*—one that encompasses their attitudes and actions about the poor, money and its use, the love of money, the treatment and use of God's creation, ideas of ownership and stewardship, and the responsibilities of the wealthy.

It is this distinctive kingdom economics by which a Kingdom Outpost operates that will be most germane to this thesis project. Economics must be understood as part of salvation, thus pointing the way to a "developmental ecclesiology." It is particularly important as part of a healthy understanding of before-afterlife salvation. Particular attention is paid to this economics and ethic as this thesis presents a church-based, kingdom theological framework for R&D, one that is manifested in the life of Kingdom Outposts.

It is the lack of a cohesive, church-based kingdom theological framework that is responsible for generating false dichotomies, well-intentioned yet harmful R&D efforts, and massive amounts of money spent and perhaps wasted by evangelicals. We need "fresh thinking on development ecclesiology" (Myers 2011, 49). I will be taking a first pass at such a theological framework for understanding the church and R&D. This project focuses on American evangelical R&D efforts. The basic premise is this: American evangelical R&D efforts most often flow from a "baptizing" of non-Christian models, philosophies, and strategies. Jayakumar Christian notes this as well:

> In his analysis of the church's role in development, Tom Sine concluded that the church has, on the whole, followed Western models of development (1981, 72). He challenged the church to examine the extent to which evangelicals have borrowed secular Western values in Christian development. (Christian 1999, 75)

In contrast to "secular Western values," this thesis will articulate biblical truths such as the following:

- The earth and its riches are not resources to be mined for profit and economic development as we see fit. The earth and its resources are a gift from God.
- We humans are not the owners of the earth and its flora, fauna, minerals, oceans, and mountains. God is the owner. We are entrusted with stewardship, not ownership.
- Wealth is not an unmitigated good, as so much R&D literature and work assumes. Wealth is a powerful tool, which can easily become an idol and a snare and a tool of oppression.
- Capitalism only requires a fair chance—a level playing field, we like to say—in order for people to develop and grow wealthier. Christ and his apostles taught that the kingdom of God requires a fair distribution of resources among the people of God, not simply fair opportunities to earn.
- Development is usually based on the concepts of ownership and the "enlightened self-interest" of capitalism. Scripture teaches not only stewardship instead of ownership but also that self-interest is opposed to the mind of Christ. "The chance workings of the free market become the 'Invisible Hand' of Adam Smith which

THE PROBLEM AND ITS SETTING

mysteriously converts private selfishness into public good" (Newbigin 1989, 206).

- The church (universal) and individual churches are sometimes seen as assets to R&D—and sometimes as obstacles to R&D. This thesis will make the case that the church—and individual churches—should in fact be the very center of R&D, and that it should operate from a different "economics" than the kingdoms of this world.

I will propose that God has given us altogether different values, and a different model and strategy, which evangelicals and their progeny ought to heed. There is a better way to address the overwhelming needs of the world's poor. There is a better way to channel the time, energy, and money of well-intentioned American evangelicals and other Christians. It is the way of Christ and his apostles.

## My Ministry Setting and Haiti as a Case Study

Lake Valley Community Church of Hot Springs, Arkansas, has a long history of both traditional mission work and R&D. The church celebrated its twentieth anniversary in June 2013, and from the beginning it has dedicated at least 10 percent of its budget to both mission and relief efforts. Today it is a community of 600–700 people, with average Sunday attendance around 500. It operates on a $1 million annual budget. I was the founding pastor of Lake Valley and have served there since June 1993.

Hot Springs is a county seat of 38,000 people. Some demographers would describe Hot Springs as a "micropolitan" community in that, while small, it has a more cosmopolitan population. It is a commercial and medical center for about 100,000 people in the broader trade area. Because it is next to a national park, there is a large federal government presence, and the town's economy depends in large part on the tourism to the park and the surrounding Ouachita National Forest and area lakes and rivers. Hot Springs has all the churches you would expect in a Bible Belt town. It is a religiously diverse community with two Roman Catholic parishes, a Greek Orthodox church, a Serbian Orthodox church, a Jewish synagogue, a Jewish hospital, a large New Age bookstore, and a sizable alternative-spirituality community. As a regional arts town, Hot Springs boasts fine-art galleries and an active music scene. Hot Springs and Garland County residents are about 90 percent white and about 8 percent African American, along with a small (2 percent) but rapidly growing Hispanic community.

Over the years, Lake Valley's mission budget has supported local Christian relief work like the Charitable Christian Medical Clinic and our Habitat for Humanity affiliate. We have built or helped build four Habitat houses. More recently, Lake Valley has been the catalyst church for organizing a ShareFest day each fall, during which area churches do hands-on projects for the city to contribute to local Christian mission efforts. Lake Valley has also sponsored events like a Dietrich Bonhoeffer play for the Arkansas Performing Arts Festival hosted in Hot Springs.

The church also has a long track record of supporting disaster relief, both financially and through hands-on work. We have sent several crews to clear rubble after Arkansas tornadoes. Following a particularly devastating tornado in northern Arkansas, we constructed a house on our church property, then moved it one hundred miles north and gave it to one of the storm victims, an older single woman. After Hurricane Katrina, we partnered with a church plant in East Bay St. Louis (near New Orleans) and sent several large teams to rebuild homes there and in the Ninth Ward.

We've been active internationally, sending short-term teams to Honduras, Guatemala, Peru, Myanmar, and Kenya for medical clinic trips, evangelism, and leadership training. We helped local Mexican leaders plant a church in an impoverished area of Monterrey, Mexico. (The church was ultimately shut down by gang violence.) We cooperated with Rotary International on a water project in Zimbabwe, with Lake Valley Community Church providing the engineering expertise for the initial project report and successful application for funding.

Finally, we financially support and mentor several church planters in the United States and Canada. Several years ago, after using the Biblical Institute of Leadership Development's (BILD) Leadership Series, we decided to focus our missions budget on three areas: R&D, church planting, and leadership training. We refer to our local ministry as "Engaging" and our US church planting work and international work as "Establishing."

In the spring of 2010, Dr. Tim Boal—pastor of a Grace Brethren church in Telford, Pennsylvania, and director of the Go2 Network—approached me with a new opportunity. I had first met Dr. Boal in the context of BILD training in Ames, Iowa. We were both deeply impacted by BILD's approach to leadership development and church-based theological training. The Grace Brethren denomination had transitioned their US church-planting ministry into the stand-alone nondenominational agency that Dr. Boal ran, the Go2 Network (Go2). Go2's mission is US church planting—specifically, to help existing US churches become involved in planting new congregations. Part of Go2's strategy was to involve US churches in international Integrated Ministries (IM). This is the Grace Brethren's nomenclature for R&D plus evangelism and church planting. The idea was that involvement in international IM helps a US church become more mission-minded. Then that church can adopt the same mission mind-set in a US setting and become involved with domestic church planting. Dr. Boal asked me to create the Integrated Ministries division for Go2.

As we discussed this opportunity with the Go2 board and our Lake Valley elders, several questions came into focus. Essentially these are the five research questions for this thesis:

1. Can a local US church go beyond sending money to missionaries and relief projects or sending teams to do short-term projects? Can it actually make a long-term, developmental difference in an international setting? If so, can we generate a reproducible pattern or system for other churches to follow?

2. What kind of partnerships and/or networks would be required to accomplish this?

3. Do the Scriptures offer a deeper understanding of what we would be trying to accomplish? In other words, is there a robust biblical theology of Integrated Ministries—that is, biblical R&D? Can something more robust than "doing good works" be defined?

4. Can we avoid reinventing the wheel? What "state of the art" thinking about Integrated Ministries already exists in the evangelical world?

5. What about the money? Can Integrated Ministries work become an "economic engine" that could provide financial support to staff an agency like the Go2 Network?

The elders of Lake Valley decided to release me to spend about half of my time and energy on this project, while I continued to pastor Lake Valley for the other half of my work.

To start, we needed a proof-of-concept initiative that could serve as a demonstration project for Integrated Ministries. By that, I mean a project that would be based on our emerging convictions about R&D and would help us test those convictions in practice. A "proof of concept" project is just that; it reveals the strengths and weaknesses of the underlying concepts and provides a laboratory for implementation efforts. This thesis uses the terms *demonstration project, pilot project*, and *proof-of-concept* interchangeably.

The project needed to be church-based. In 2010 we understood that to mean that it would (1) be rooted in a US church, yet (2) it would somehow strengthen the international church while doing Integrated Ministries. For our pilot project, Lake Valley would serve as the US church. We already had contacts in many countries, as did the Go2 Network, so where would we start?

On January 12, 2010, a massive earthquake hit Port-au-Prince, Haiti. In a country of just over ten million people, at least 200,000 were killed and another 300,000 injured. Millions more were displaced and homeless in the aftermath (Farmer 2011, 118). An already ineffective government was devastated by the destruction in the capital city and essentially became nonfunctioning. Haiti was already the poorest country in the western hemisphere, with about half of its population living on $2 a day or less (Farmer 2011, 60). Over 9,000 NGOs were already active in Haiti, earning it the derogatory nickname "The Republic of NGOs" (Kristoff and Panarelli 2010).

It has been estimated that there are fewer than 100,000 tax-paying jobs in Haiti—and that was before the earthquake. Unemployment has been estimated to be as high as 50 percent, though such statistics are difficult to verify in Haiti (World Bank 2013). The country survives economically on a combination of international aid and money transfers from the Haitian diaspora in the United States and other countries. The litany of problems before the earthquake was already daunting: deforestation, poor education, a massive brain drain, a devastated agricultural sector, and ineffective religion (Farmer 2011). The country is traditionally Roman Catholic, with a growing Protestant base that some now estimate at nearing 40 percent of the population. And as one Haitian told me, "We're 60 percent Catholic, 40 percent Protestant, and 100 percent Voodoo." Voodoo superstition and ignorance still abound, with Protestant pastors reporting significant encounters with principalities and powers.

In August 2010, Dr. Tim Boal and I accompanied the New York City Leadership Center (NYCLC) on a scouting trip to Port-au-Prince. Go2 already enjoyed a long relationship with the NYCLC, an organization that offers training and mobilization for Christian leaders (both in ministry and in the marketplace) in the greater New York City area. Because of the large Haitian community in New York, the NYCLC was already involved with the Haitian evangelical diaspora. After the earthquake, it focused on Haiti as one of its primary Global Initiatives.

At the time of our scouting trip, eight months after the earthquake, only about 2 percent of the debris had been removed. Little to no reconstruction had taken place. Some 1.5 million Haitians were still homeless and living outdoors or in tents. While billions of dollars of international government aid had been promised, very little had been delivered, according to an online report by the NYCLC. Even as I started this thesis a little more than two years later, much international aid was still being withheld primarily over concerns about government and social corruption. As of late 2012, Canada was actively considering cutting off aid to Haiti—in spite of a large Haitian community in Montreal—due to concerns over misappropriation of funds and little demonstrable progress since the earthquake:

> Canadian Minister of International Co-operation Julian Fantino has reiterated his concern that Haiti's bid to become self-sustaining isn't happening quickly enough, three years after a

devastating earthquake struck the Caribbean nation, killing an estimated 300,000 people and leaving more than 1.5 million homeless.

"We remain concerned with the slow progress of development in Haiti, in large part due to weakness in their governing institutions," Fantino said in a ministerial statement released on Tuesday. (CBC News—Montreal, January 8, 2013)

During that trip I was asked—along with Mr. Nelson Peters, a Go2 supporter—to share our findings with a focus on emerging leaders. This report was not meant to be a programmatic statement for Go2's Integrated Ministries. Rather, we were trying to support the NYCLC and their Rebuild Haiti Initiative, while scouting for Go2's proof-of-concept project. NYCLC also has a close partnership with World Vision, who helped arrange the trip, and World Vision at the time was also trying to formulate its long-term earthquake response. Here is a summary of our report to the NYCLC:

Any long-term solutions to Haiti's situation will not come from the outside by trying to give hope TO Haiti, but will come from within as a Haiti with hope emerges. The long-term strategic key, then, is to identify and develop Haiti's future leaders who will lead with hope and vision. Community leaders are needed—whether leading in business, society, or the church. Before us is the opportunity to do much more than triage in the stricken capital of Port-au-Prince. We have a redemptive opportunity to see God's kingdom advance and a new nation emerge. Our mission is to rebuild Haiti from within for the glory of God.

Our strategy is to:

1. Identify promising young Haitian leaders—that is, followers of Christ with a demonstrated potential for learning and leading, identified in concert with indispensable local leaders and networks, working outside of government agencies. We are looking for potential marketplace leaders who can be equipped to lead both in society and in the church.

2. Train and develop their character and capacity as both business and kingdom leaders. We will train young leaders to train other leaders, both in the marketplace and in the church of Haiti. This training needs to proceed from a holistic kingdom vision of church and society. They will experience development in character, skills, and theology.

3. Resource them for success in building a civil society in Haiti, thus advancing the kingdom of God. This includes such things as introductions into business networks outside of Haiti, access to credentialing when necessary, access to financing and funding for seed money to develop exportable products and microbusinesses, personal mentoring, etc.

The report identified some of the challenges and roadblocks that would have to be overcome for the

NYCLC's Rebuild Haiti initiative, and then it suggested nine action steps to more deeply understand the situation there. In particular we noted that we (that is, the US citizens on the trip) did not understand the situation very well and should be extremely cautious about promising immediate deliverables, or even in pretending to know what services need to be delivered. Further, we noted the complete breakdown of infrastructure in the Port-au-Prince area—a challenge that should not be underestimated while attempting to implement an R&D program in Haiti.

It should be noted that the perspective we had at the time was not yet the fully developed perspective presented in this thesis. Our strategies and understanding of the issues would change during the course of the HaitiCure project, which is presented in chapter four of this thesis.

Before long, it became clear that Haiti should be the focus of Go2 and Lake Valley's demonstration project. It was close to the United States. It was the poorest country in the western hemisphere, now suffering a major disaster, with a large diaspora population in the United States, including the New York City area. In September 2010 the NYCLC conducted their first Movement Day in New York City. Part of that day was a breakout track called the Rebuild Haiti Initiative. Go2 helped sponsor Movement Day, and I was involved in the Rebuild Haiti track. During Movement Day, I met Pastor Mullery Jean-Pierre of Beraca Baptist Church in Brooklyn, New York, and heard him speak of his desire to train Haitian pastors both in New York and in Haiti. He also shared his church's plans to initiate church planting and business development in Léogâne,

Haiti, which was the epicenter of the earthquake. He was already in conversations with BILD about church-based leadership training in New York.

Following Movement Day, the NYCLC published its mission and vision statement for its Rebuild Haiti Initiative. They had several five-year goals, including a goal "to enlist 50 U.S. pastors to train 1,000 Haitian pastors in Christian ethics and practical theological skills." Further, they envisioned as one of the six projected outcomes that "hundreds of American pastors and churches [would build] significant partnerships with churches in Haiti."

The NYCLC has a small staff primarily responsible for convening and mobilizing others. At the time, the NYCLC was beginning to envision partnership with Go2 and Lake Valley Community Church, in which NYCLC would deliver pastoral training and involve US partner churches. Of course, as the project unfolded and as our understanding of the role indigenous leaders would play in large-scale, church-based theological training developed, these assumptions and plans changed.

In addition, I came to understand my role as that of an apostolic leader. By this term, I am referring to the kind of leadership gifts mentioned in Ephesians 4:11–12 and 1 Corinthians 12:27–31. Apostolic leaders are men and women who are sent across racial, cultural, and geographical boundaries and use the same model as the apostle Paul and his teams. These leaders are entrusted with a stewardship of the gospel for the planting and strengthening of local churches. Their parental influence on these churches helps to bind networks of churches together.

When I was helping plant Lake Valley in 1993, I was fresh out of seminary, but I had already planted another church during my engineering days. At that time, when I thought of leaders in the New Testament, I only thought of elders. I was wrong about that. There are a variety of leaders in the New Testament. Just prior to the project described in this thesis, and during the course of this project, I was developing a fresh understanding of myself as one of those apostolic leaders described in Ephesians 4:11. I was learning how I should work with my local church, other local churches, and other apostolic leaders. Together with the elders of Lake Valley, I had wrestled with this concept just enough by fall 2010 to take the first step of application.

The elders of Lake Valley made the decision to share me with Go2 in October 2010. I was to start this new venture on January 1, 2011. Lake Valley would continue to pay my full salary, and Go2 would raise $25,000 to cover a year's worth of expenses. At Lake Valley, we shifted half of my income from our compensation budget to our establishing budget. During this time we also began familiarizing ourselves with the evangelical literature on R&D. When *Helping Hurts* by Steve Corbett and Brian Fikkert became the gateway piece that opened up conversation in both evangelical and marketplace circles, as detailed in chapter three.

At this same time, our church-based theological education effort at Lake Valley was intensifying. BILD International had achieved accreditation for their Antioch School of Church Planting and Leadership Development (Antioch School). We had been using their training materials for twelve years to great effect for our own leadership development needs. Three men from Lake Valley and a fourth local pastor enrolled in the Antioch School to earn master's degrees in theology. This work was starting to contribute to the theological understanding detailed in this thesis, especially as we worked through the Antioch School's biblical theology curriculum.

While we have made a lot of progress as a theological learning community, our development of a biblical understanding of R&D is recent. The next chapter outlines my current thinking and theology and presents a storied, church-based theological framework for R&D. This framework is already informing our decision making about Lake Valley's R&D efforts, and it is shaping our understanding of core theological concepts such as salvation, the church, and God's kingdom.

This, then, is the rationale for my thesis. Current evangelical and secular R&D efforts are often inefficient. Often they are actually harmful. Of greater concern is that evangelical efforts too often are rooted in a secular paradigm of R&D, rather than a biblical paradigm. Churches and their leaders are in desperate need—whether they know it or not—of an effective biblical theology to inform their actions and initiatives as they seek to meet the needs of the poor and oppressed. Without a doubt there are current best practices and approaches that are consistent with the biblical paradigm. We will look at some of these in chapter three. However, it would be a mistake to simply baptize Western, secular approaches to the staggering problems of human poverty, injustice, and suffering. We need a sure foundation in the way of Christ and his apostles. From that sure footing, we can integrate what we are learning about R&D into a more faithful and effective approach. It is easy to guess that Jesus' way will be somewhat counterintuitive, counter-cultural, and counter to the way of the world. But it is the only way that offers Christians a rock instead of sand on which to build the R&D house.

# CHAPTER TWO

# FRAMEWORK FOR A CHURCH-BASED THEOLOGY OF RELIEF AND DEVELOPMENT

Relief and development is notably absent from the Bible. At least, R&D as we usually define it and frame it is absent. This would seem to be problematic for writing a biblical theology of R&D. But the story of God's mission and promises actually has much to say about the relief of the poor; the development of sustainable economies; the use and abuse of wealth, privilege, work, and money; and the vision of *shalom* for the planet and its civilizations. I will be sketching out a case for a different definition and framing of R&D. It is a vision of Kingdom Outposts, these new communities of Jesus, established in the apostles' teaching and practicing a distinctive economics.

## My Theological Pre-Understanding

I'd like to start by stating my own assumptions and perspective because the theology that follows is unavoidably shaped by them. I grew up in a Baptist family in the American South. Both of these facts have theological implications. My religion was a settled frontier revivalism. It focused on adult conversion for an afterlife salvation, as well as conservative Christian morality. I've moved from that world and approach, but its emphasis on mission, on the local church, and on a distinctive lifestyle have stayed with me. It was in many ways a very different stream than the Princetonian-fundamentalist-evangelical stream of American Christianity. Much of the evangelical literature that will be reviewed in this thesis flowed from this academic evangelical stream, but I will be writing from a more Anabaptist, church-based stream. I believe theology should be done at the highest level possible: the local church. The mind of Christ resides in the body of Christ filled with the Spirit of Christ, as the apostle Paul reminded the Corinthian church (see 1 Corinthians 2:16).

Growing up in the American South shaped me in another important way. In the book *The American Idea of Success*, Richard Huber develops at some length the American focus and myth surrounding "success," defined as making money—and lots of it. And yet he exempts the American South from his study:

> This study has excluded the South for good reasons. Up North and out West the idea of success had taken hold. It was a goal pursued in the city, not on the farm. The idea of success concentrated, in the beginning, in a mercantile-commercial world. Later, it embraced manufacturing and finance... [The South, after the Civil War] was shattered by economic disintegration and hurt pride. With its crumbling plantation economy and *predominantly agrarian values*,

it was in no condition to compete with applied science and technology... What was this Southern "differentness"? It contained values which were counterproductive to industrialism. Comforted by a Lost Cause and a Plantation Legend, southern 'differentness' was expressed in a European deference for social distinctions, graciously formed manners between men and women and children and adults, a smoldering mood of defeat, anxieties about the Negro and the meaning of work, tribal customs and dialects, the fantasies of both suffering as the victim and surviving as an executioner. However similar the South may have been to the nation in other respects, too many generalizations about success do not comfortably correspond to the southern experience or its values. We have, therefore, omitted a consideration of the South from this study. (Huber 1987, 31–32, emphasis added)

When it comes to issues of poverty and economic development, basic mind-sets and values about wealth, success, land, jobs, work, debt, and money come into play. American evangelical thought-leadership tends to come from a modern, Northern industrial perspective. It is a perspective focused on efficiency, scalability, speed, profit, innovation, technique, and technology. I'll be writing from the base of a Southern agrarian perspective, which has been "industrialized" by my education. That agrarian perspective is more focused on land and land stewardship, tradition, family, clan, and tribe. From an industrial perspective, the American South has been an "underdeveloped nation" that lags behind the North and West.

Wendell Berry is perhaps the foremost essayist writing today on these "predominantly agrarian values." Berry is a Kentucky farmer and English professor at the University of Kentucky—as well as a Christian. He sums up the differences between an agrarian and an industrial perspective this way:

> I believe that this contest between industrialism and agrarianism now defines the most fundamental human difference, for it divides not just two nearly opposite concepts of agriculture and land use, but also two nearly opposite ways of understanding ourselves, our fellow creatures, and our world.
>
> The way of industrialism is the way of the machine. To the industrial mind, a machine is not merely an instrument for doing work or amusing ourselves or making war; it is an explanation of the world and its life... Because industrialism cannot understand living things except as machines, and can grant them no value that is not utilitarian, it conceives of farming and forestry as forms of mining; it cannot use the land without abusing it...
>
> Industrialism begins with technological invention...
>
> I said a while ago that to agrarianism farming is the proper use and care of an immeasurable gift. The shortest way to understand this, I suppose, is the religious way. Among the commonplaces of the Bible, for example, are the admonitions that

the world was made and approved by God, that it belongs to Him, and that its good things come to us from Him as gifts. Beyond those ideas is the idea that the whole Creation exists only by participating in the life of God, sharing in His being, breathing His breath...

Such thoughts seem strange to us now, and what has estranged us from them is our economy. The industrial economy could not have been derived from such thoughts any more than it could have been derived from the golden rule. If we believed that the existence of the world is rooted in mystery and in sanctity, then we would have a different economy. (Berry 2003, 144–146)

Agrarianism does not mean that everyone should be a farmer. Agrarianism is not nostalgia for a sentimental vision of farm life, romantically stripped of its hard work and barnyard smells. Nor does it reject science or technology out of hand. Note the quote below from Ellen F. Davis. Davis is not a farmer; she is a professor of Bible in Practical Theology at Duke Divinity School, having previously taught at Union Theological Seminary and Yale Divinity School. She defines an agrarian perspective this way in her important study *Scripture, Culture, and Agriculture*:

Agrarianism is a way of thinking and ordering life in community that is based on the health of the land and of living creatures. Often out of step with the prevailing values of wealth, technology, and political and military domination, the mind-set and practices that constitute agrarianism have been marginalized by the powerful within most "history-making" cultures across time, including that of ancient Israel. Yet, *agrarianism is the way of thinking predominant among the biblical writers*, who very often do not represent the interests of the powerful. The sheer pervasiveness of their appreciation and concern for the health of the land is the single most important point of this study. (Davis 2009, 1, emphasis added)

She also notes the association of the American South with agrarian thinking, and takes into account its sinful history as well:

Over the last three generations, agrarian thought and values have been given their fullest articulation in the nearly three millennia of agrarian writing; it is now clear that *this is a comprehensive way of viewing the world and the human place in it*. (Davis 2009, 1, emphasis added)

Because the agrarian history of the United States bears the taint and curse of slavery, contemporary agrarians are challenged to acknowledge that aspect of our history, to disavow its presumptions about human worth, and also to recognize its current consequences including the movement of large parts of Southern rural populations to Northern cities and the increase of suburbanism and urban poverty. (Davis 2009, footnote 2, 181)

This thesis will use the term *agrarian* to refer to this "comprehensive way of viewing the world," in distinction from an industrial perspective. Hallmarks of the agrarian view include seeing that the Creator-creature relationship makes the earth and its inhabitants sacred; viewing this world and its creatures as gifts from the Creator for the care of humanity; believing that these gifts must be stewarded for one another and for future generations; and understanding that science and technology are valuable when included in a larger agrarian perspective, but destructive when allowed to frame reality in reductionist ways.

What do an agrarian perspective and agrarian values have to do with theology? What Wendell Berry calls "the commonplaces of the Bible," regarding land and economy, are in fact not commonplace at all in evangelical theologies regarding R&D. Assumptions about success and development goals in evangelical R&D literature more closely adhere to what Berry calls "industrialism." I believe our industrial perspective blinds us to one of the major themes of the Bible: land (which will be presented in this chapter). Land as a biblical theme is so much more than an eschatological trigger about the supposedly unfulfilled promise to Abraham. Land is about economics, stewardship, worship, peace, and the relief of the poor among God's people. Land is about salvation:

> The Bible itself is primarily concerned with the issue of being displaced and yearning for a place. Indeed, the Bible promises precisely what the modern world denies... In what follows, *land* will be used to refer to *actual earthly turf* where people can be safe and secure, where meaning and well-being are enjoyed without pressure or coercion. *Land* will also be used in a *symbolic*

sense, as the Bible itself uses it, to express the wholeness of joy and well-being characterized by social coherence and personal ease in prosperity, security, and freedom. (Brueggemann 1977, 2)

R&D is usually not a category or subcategory of systematic theology. Evangelicals often use the phrase "mercy and justice" to stand for a distinctly biblical view of R&D. But I'm not sure we know where to put such a concern in our systematics. Does it belong in ecclesiology, missiology, soteriology, or eschatology? This chapter proposes a different approach, one that's distinct from systematic theology. Yet if R&D must reside in a single category of systematic theology—in reality, it bears on all four categories just mentioned—perhaps it should be soteriology. R&D overlaps significantly with our normal concerns in soteriology. Rightly understood, R&D can fill out the before-afterlife part of our soteriology that is often missing.

Further, what we normally call systematic theology, I understand as historical theology of a philosophic type. Every church in every time and in every culture has to do contextualized theology—that is, theology-in-culture. What we have received as systematic theology made for outstanding theology-in-culture in the context of premodern Europe and modern America. There is much to learn from it as historical theology. But I do not believe it should be enthroned as the last word in theology. In fact, I believe it is inadequate for our rapidly shifting post-Christendom era. As Dr. Richard Lints commented in one of my doctor of ministry cohort gatherings, "Systematics—the form is an artifact of historical theology. It is a framework that no longer resonates" (from class notes, March 2006, Gordon-Conwell Seminary).

Rather, we must do what those premodern Reformers did: go back to the sources. Revisit the DNA of our faith. Refresh our memories in the story of God's redemptive mission. And then face our world as it is now and live out the message of his kingdom.

I believe the Scriptures are inspired by God for God's people. It is a community-shaping book. And it's a book that was written and shaped by that same community. It's a book that is meant to be heard by the community, argued over by the community, and lived out in community. Reading it well is not an academic exercise in any sense of that term. It is a political exercise undertaken by the community of Jesus followers. The political concerns raised by our reading include issues of community boundaries, community ethics and practice, use of power and violence, money and its use and abuse, relationships with outsiders, and the values of the good life as it is defined by that community.

In other words, it's Our Book. It doesn't belong to everyone. It doesn't belong to every group or culture. It belongs to those who follow the King of the Book as he builds his kingdom. It does not offer general principles to be applied by anyone who happens to read a few verses. You have to learn to read it, and you learn it by living in the community of the Book and being trained by life in that community. It is not validated by any appeal to any outside sources or foundations of knowledge. Its only apologetic is the public life of a community that follows the hero of the Book, the Messiah, by hearing his message and believing it—that is, by living it.

## Theological Method and Themes

Rather than locate R&D on a systematic theology map, I will use a different map—a biblical theology map. The term *biblical theology* has been used to describe very different approaches to theology. I appreciate Dr. Richard Lints's use of the term *storied theology* (Lints 1993), as this is how I understand biblical theology. Biblical theology takes the overarching story and all the individual stories of the Bible as a cohesive presentation that sets its own categories—or better, its own themes. Identifying these themes requires reading the story in community, and in a community that includes disparate people. Others will see themes that our own pre-understanding screened out. As themes are identified by the community, they should take priority over any of our prior systematizing. Systematizing is proper and inevitable. However, our systems should always be subject to the story and its own themes, *semper reformandi*. Biblical theology, as I understand it, regards the overarching story and the individual stories as the DNA of our faith. I believe the themes of this story should not simply be *informing* our agendas, but *setting* our agendas.

During the first cohort meeting of my doctor of ministry track, we witnessed an interesting convergence of theological method as Jeff Reed, Dr. Walter Kaiser, and Dr. Richard Lints discussed theological method with one another and with the cohort. Jeff Reed presented the following synthesis of the discussion:

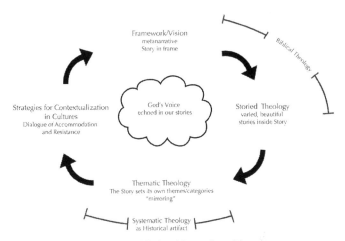

**Figure 1.** Jeff Reed and Richard Lints: Four Movements of Storied, Church-Based Theology

As summarized by this figure, I will read the Scriptures from a narrative promise/covenant framework, reading the stories of the storied theology, and doing thematic theology by tracing three of the major themes of the story as it applies to R&D. The project presented later in chapter four, HaitiCure, is an attempt at the last of the four moves depicted in this figure—that is, contextualization in cultures.

So there is a framework of the story that defines the people of God and their book. But this idea is not beyond dispute. Even among those who believe there is a cohesive framework, there is disagreement on how to characterize this framework. The framework I have adopted in this chapter was influenced by several teachers, both in person and in print—including Dr. Walter Kaiser and his "promise theology" (Kaiser 1987); Dr. Richard Lints and the "storied theology" of promise and fulfillment (1993); Dr. John Sailhamer and his distinction between text and event and the kingdom "stitching" of the Pentateuch (Sailhamer 1992); Jeff Reed and his church-based reading of Acts and the Pauline epistles (Reed 1992, 2009); Dr. Stanley Hauerwas and his ethics (Hauerwas 1991); John Howard Yoder's understanding of politics (Yoder 1994); N. T. Wright's work on the setting of "second-Temple Judaism" and Jesus (Wright 2008); Christopher Wright's work on the mission of God (Wright 1990, 2006, 2010); and Lesslie Newbigin's perspective on pluralism and the gospel (Newbigin 1989).

Kaiser has characterized this framework as "the Promise-Plan of God" (Kaiser 1987, 83) and traces its development through the narrative as the promise made to Eve, Shem, Abraham, Isaac, Jacob, David, and the prophets (Kaiser 1987, 89). Christopher Wright makes essentially the same assertion, using the word *covenant*:

> Covenant is one of several major components in Israel's essential theological self-understanding. And the sequence of covenants in the canonical narrative offers us *one* fruitful way of presenting the grand narrative [of the Old Testament]. (Wright 2006, 325)

He traces the "grand narrative" through the covenants with Noah, Abraham, Moses, David, and the new covenant (Wright 2006, 326ff.).

The framework that follows will be built through eight major promises (or covenants) of Scripture:

1. Creation and the Promise in Eden
2. The Promise to Abraham
3. The Mosaic Covenant
4. The Early Prophets and the Promise to David

5. The Latter Prophets and the Promised Day of the Lord
6. Fulfillment in Christ
7. Extension through Kingdom Outposts
8. Final Consummation

Just to note, in the Old Testament I will largely ignore the Writings, focusing instead on the Torah and the Prophets. This is because it is the Torah and the Prophets that carry the framework forward. My concern in this chapter is to establish the three themes—God, his people, his land—within the framework provided by the Torah, the Prophets, and the New Testament. Several books of the Writings do indeed provide illustrations of these themes, as well as further teaching on them. For instance, the book of Ruth illustrates the faithful use of land and wealth to benefit the poor, in Boaz and his treatment of Ruth. (I'm using the traditional Jewish categorization of Ruth as part of the Writings.) Psalm 104 says in poetic language what the Torah says in prose: God owns the land, not us. But the argument of this thesis is carried forward largely by the Torah and the Prophets.

I propose to trace three major biblical themes through the eight major narratives or promises detailed above. A few key passages will be considered from each of these narrative sections. These passages will inform our developing understanding of a distinctive kingdom approach to R&D. The three themes are as follows:

1. God, his character, and his gracious love toward all his creation, evidenced by his care to feed us— that is, his hospitality

2. The people of God, not as the source of R&D efforts but as the *locus* of R&D living

3. The land, God's wise provision for his people for salvation, freedom, sustainable living, wealth, the care of the poor, economics, R&D, and the arena of blessing

The following framework is developed in canonical, or diachronic, order from Genesis to Revelation. However, my personal understanding does not begin in Genesis. It begins with Jesus and his apostles, particularly as recorded in the Luke–Acts narrative. I understand Luke's two-part narrative to be his encapsulation of the apostle Paul's gospel and missionary methods. Paul argues in Galatians that he learned his gospel from the risen Christ himself (Galatians 1–2). During his first missionary journey (as recorded in Acts), Paul preaches his gospel to a largely Jewish audience; on his second journey, he preaches to a skeptical Greek audience:

Compare Paul's sermon in the Jewish synagogue in Pisidian Antioch in Acts 13:16-41 with his speech before the Areopagus in Athens in Acts 17:22-31. Both addresses have a common ultimate purpose—to introduce his listeners to Jesus. But the conceptual frameworks are very different. In the first, before a Jewish audience, Paul speaks of "the *God* of [this] people *Israel*" and describes how God had overthrown the Canaanites and "gave [them] their *land* [as an] inheritance" (Acts 13:17, 19, emphasis added). In the second, before a Gentile audience, Paul speaks of "the *God* who made the world and everything in it," and describes how this God "[made from one man *every nation of mankind* to live on all the face of the earth]" (Acts 17:24, 26, emphasis added). (Wright 2006, 393)

Wright uses the following diagram to capture the three themes of the framework of Paul's sermon in Acts 13:

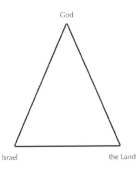

**Figure 2.** Paul's Pisidian Antioch Sermon

Paul's sermon in Acts 17, building on this basic thematic framework, extends that framework to include his mission to the Gentiles:

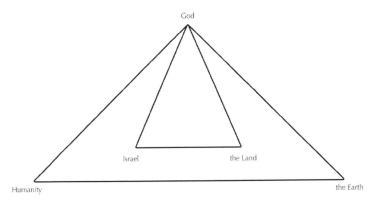

**Figure 3.** Paul's Athens Sermon

This, of course, frames Paul's ministry and his message: the promises to Israel are fulfilled in the appointed Messiah Jesus, and the blessings of those promises now extend to all people, Jew and Greek, throughout the whole earth.

Christopher Wright, Old Testament professor and director of international ministries for John Stott Ministries, is well aware that there are many proposals about what the Bible is "all about" (Wright 2006, 29). His book *The Mission of God* is structured around these three themes we see in Paul's gospel: God, his people, his land. Wright sees these themes as carrying the narrative of God's salvation, of his plan to set the world right and redeem humanity and all creation—that is, God's mission. And Wright sees them as rooted first in Jesus and his teachings:

> I take some encouragement in persisting with my claim from the words of the risen Jesus as recorded in Luke 24. First to the two on the road to Emmaus and then later to the rest of the disciples, Jesus made himself as Messiah the focus of the whole canon of the Hebrew Scriptures that we now call the Old Testament (vv. 27, 44). So we are accustomed to speaking of the christological focus or center of the Bible. For Christians the whole Bible revolves around the person of Christ.
>
> Jesus went on, however, beyond his *messianic* centering of the Old Testament Scriptures to their *missional* thrust as well.
>
> [Then he opened their minds to understand the Scriptures, and said to them, "Thus it is

written, that the Christ should suffer and on the third day rise from the dead, and that repentance and forgiveness of sins should be proclaimed in his name to all nations, beginning from Jerusalem.]" (Luke 24:45-47)

Jesus' whole sentence comes under the rubric "[Thus it] is written."... Luke tells us that with these words Jesus "opened their minds [to] understand the Scriptures," or as we might put it, he was setting their hermeneutical orientation and agenda. The proper way for disciples of the crucified and risen Jesus to read their Scriptures is messianically and *missionally*. (Wright 2006, 29–30)

Wright defines *missional* as "something that is related to or characterized by mission, or has the qualities, attributes or dynamics of mission" (2006, 24). He describes mission this way:

It will be immediately clear from my reminis-cences above that I am dissatisfied with popular use of the word mission (or more commonly in the United States, missions) solely in relation to human endeavors of various kinds. I do not at all question the validity of Christian active engagement in mission, but I do want to argue throughout this book for the theological priority of God's mission. *Fundamentally, our mission (if it is biblically informed and validated) means our committed participation as God's people, at God's invitation and command, in God's own mission within the history of God's world for the redemption of God's creation.* That is how I usually answer when I am asked how I would define mission. Our mission flows from and participates in the mission of God. (Wright 2006, 22–23)

Thus, as we trace the development of the themes of God, people, and land, we are tracing the story of salvation—that is, God's mission with his people to redeem the whole earth (land). The framework, then, consists of the promises that God made to his people about their land. The specific promises reveal in increasing detail the nature of his salvation mission. These promises (promises 1–5 in this thesis) eventually find their fulfillment in Christ (promise 6), and they extend to all humanity through Kingdom Outposts (promise 7). God's mission will someday find its final consummation at Jesus' second advent (promise 8).

It has always been obvious to evangelicals that God's salvation includes the themes of a holy God saving a people for himself. But what is this theme of land all about? Why was it part of Jesus' self-understanding as Messiah and such a major—if often overlooked—part of Paul's gospel? Brueggemann explains it like this:

And if God has to do with Israel in a special way, as he surely does, he has to do with land as a historical place in a special way. It will no longer do to talk about Yahweh and his people but we must speak about Yahweh and his people *and his land.* (Brueggemann 1982, 6)

Consider this from Christopher Wright:

> The promise of land [to Israel] was an essential part of the patriarchal *election* tradition. The land was the goal of the exodus *redemption* tradition. The maintenance of the *covenant* relationship and the security of life in the land were bound together. Divine *judgment* eventually meant expulsion from the land, until the restored *relationship* was symbolized in the return to the land...
>
> For the Israelite, living with his family on his allotted share of YHWH's land, the land itself was the proof of his membership of God's people and the focus of his practical response to God's grace. (Wright 2006, 292)

*Election, redemption, covenant, judgment, restored relationship, grace*—these are salvation words. In the Old Testament, the land not only represented salvation; it *was* salvation. But what are we to make of the theme of land when we turn to the New Testament? This third theme, does it disappear? More from Christopher Wright:

> It is true that we must take into account the radical newness of the era of salvation history inaugurated in the New Testament. We are not Old Testament Israelites living within a theocratic covenant bound by Old Testament law. So, for example, when we take a theme such as the land of Israel we do need to recognize the typological-prophetic hermeneutic by which the New Testament sees the fulfillment of all it signified for Israel as now fulfilled for Christians by *being in Christ*. The

land of Palestine as territory and turf is no longer theologically (or eschatologically) significant in the New Testament. *Nevertheless, as I have argued elsewhere in detail, the paradigmatic force of the socioeconomic legislation that governed Israel's life in the land still has ethical and missional relevance for Christians—in the church and in society.* (Wright 2006, 304–305, emphasis added)

Brueggemann makes the same point by referencing the work of W. D. Davies:

[Davies] concludes that in the history of Christianity the land as a central theme has been (a) rejected, (b) spiritualized, (c) treated historically, and (d) presented sacramentally. But the major thrust of Davies's study is to stress that in early Christianity the theme of land was displaced by the person of Jesus Christ.

The present discussion owes much to Davies's work. However, it is here urged that the land theme is more central than Davies believes and that it has not been so fully spiritualized as he concludes...

The most primitive and central image of this contrast is the image of kingdom, Kingdom of God and kingdom of this world. The primary claim is that a new kingdom has come (Mark 1:14-15; cf. Rev. 11:15). The theme of "kingdom" is crucial for our consideration. It clearly includes among its nuances the idea of historical, political, physical realm, that is, land...

... In the Old Testament the resurrection motif is undoubtedly expressed as the call to exiles to leave exile and to return to the land.

Thus crucifixion/resurrection echoes the dialectic of *possessed land lost/exiles en route to the land of promise.* Jesus embodies precisely what Israel has learned about land: being without land makes it possible to trust the promise of it, while grasping land is the sure way to lose it. The powerful are called to dispossession. The powerless are called to power. The landed are called to *homelessness.* The landless are given a *new home.* Both are called to discipleship, to be "in Christ," to submit to the one who has become the embodiment of the new land. (Brueggemann 1977, 170, 180)

Fulfillment of the land theme in Christ and the extension of the land theme through the apostolic mission to establish Kingdom Outposts, then, is the culmination of the narrative theology that follows. The theme of land, its purpose, and its use by the people of God teach us a biblical vision of R&D. God is concerned from the beginning that people have food, shelter, and clothing. He gives us the land—the earth—that all may be cared for and that we may care for one another. Jesus is the fulfillment of all that was anticipated for God's people and his land in the Old Testament. Through his apostles, the spread of the churches—that is, Kingdom Outposts—is the kingdom extension of that fulfillment.

# The Gospel of the Kingdom
## 1. Creation and the Promise in Eden (Genesis 1–3)

In just three chapters the Torah sketches out both the Creator's vision for humanity and our failure to enter into that vision. The Lord speaks the universe into existence and orders our earth so that it is a hospitable home for humans. We're immediately told that we are created "in his own image," and that we are to "be fruitful," "subdue" the earth, and "have dominion" over every living thing (Genesis 1:26–31). In recent years, scholars have documented this language of image, subduing, and dominion as ancient Near Eastern kingdom language:

> Across the ancient world, the image of God did the work of God on the earth. In the Israelite context as portrayed in the Hebrew Bible, people are in the image of God in that they embody his qualities and do his work. They are symbols of his presence and act on his behalf as his representatives. (Walton 2006, 212)

It is the language of a high king who is giving a subordinate king and queen authority over part of his kingdom. The new king and queen are meant to rule in the high king's image—that is, according to his wishes, policies, and goals (Blocher 1984, 86). And while the language of subduing and dominion has been used to justify abusing the earth, this tendency represents a gross misreading of the Creator's intention. The Lord is delighted with his creation; he declares it "good." In fact, it is "very good" (Genesis 1:31). Yet, as we see in Genesis 2, the work of developing and caring for it remains unfinished. This work is delegated to humanity, along with the power and authority to accomplish it in God's image.

Further, in loving hospitality, the Lord provides food for humanity: "Behold, I have given you every plant yielding seed that is on the face of all the earth, and every tree with seed in its fruit. You shall have them for food" (1:29). It is all too easy to read past this familiar verse. Here at the very outset of the Torah, at the very beginning of the metanarrative of the entire Bible, we see the theological priority of having food to eat! This will, of course, become a major theme in the Torah, along with the related themes of plenty, famine, hoarding, manna, and a land flowing with milk and honey.

Genesis 2 is an even more focused creation narrative—a narrative focused mostly on eating. The Lord himself plants a garden for us. He waters it with a river flowing out of Eden. He puts the man (Heb., *adam*), who was made from humus or clay (Heb., *adamah*), in the garden to "work it and keep it" (2:15). Sometimes translated "till it and tend it," these verbs are not actually agricultural terms (Davis 2009, 29). They are terms used that refer to a craftsman working on (or with) any material, while carefully taking into account the properties of that material. These terms convey the sense of serving the material's needs by improving or developing it somehow. The material's inherent worth must be respected by the work done on it.

So we humans are made from humus—*adam* from *adamah*. We come from the land or the "fertile soil" of earth. We have dominion, but not for destruction. Rather, at the very beginning of our story, we are in need of food, and our Creator gives us the plants we will need, the garden in which to cultivate them, and a river to water it. We are asked to work with the land respectfully and faithfully, according to God's wishes and design. The work will be good and the work will be light. This is the hospitality of God:

> Adam comes to Eden as a protector, answerable for the well-being of the precious thing that he did not make; he is to be an observer, mindful of limits that are built into the created order as both inescapable and fitting. The biblical writer does not subscribe to the fantasy that our society has embraced as an ideal—that human ingenuity runs up against physical limits only in order to overcome them. Rather... we encounter [the earth] as a fellow creature to be respected and even revered. (Davis 2009, 31)

And this work with the Creator, to care for and work his land in his image, is set in place before the fall. It is important to note that work is not a consequence of our unbelief. It is part of God's good vision for us and for the earth. Eve is given to Adam as his crucial ally in this work (2:18). If they respect the limits God places on them—"of the tree of the knowledge of good and evil you shall not eat" (2:17)—trust the Creator's wisdom, and tend the garden, then all will be well. This is purposeful work, which provides the first humans a way to love God and each other. Good work that ensures there is enough to eat. A garden in which to live is provided. Here there is no shame, no hiding, no death. Instead there is *shalom*. It is paradise:

An agrarian reading of the Bible thus forces the de-specialization of one's thoughts about agriculture. With equal force it de-specializes one's thoughts about religion. It does this simply by seeing that the Bible is not a book only about "spirituality" or getting to Heaven, but is also a practical book about the good use of the land and creatures as a religious practice, and about the abuse of the land and creatures as a kind of blasphemy. (Wendell Berry, in the foreword to Davis 2009, x)

However, the first humans fail to rule over one of the creatures over which they have authority and dominion: the serpent. They listen to a creature instead of the Creator. Eve is deceived and Adam willfully rebels. They become greedy and ignore the limits. The forbidden tree looks like good food, beautiful and nourishing. Eve chooses the lust of her eyes, Adam chooses the lust of his flesh (i.e., Eve), and they both fall victim to the pride of life—by eating! Eating and sex are two of the most— maybe *the* most—sensual and spiritual things a person does. Both activities are meant to tie us closer to one another and to our Maker. But we allowed them to drive us apart. Thus the vision is ruined and the consequences follow immediately.

A promise—actually, a threat—is given to the serpent: there will be war between its seed and the seed of the woman. Where there was meant to be loving, wise rule and dominion, now there will be strife. While the serpent will wound the woman's seed, he will deal the serpent a fatal blow. Eve will indeed be "fruitful and multiply," but now her pain will be "multiplied." Adam will indeed "work and keep" the fertile soil, but now its fertility will work against him, bringing forth thorns and thistles. His work will be painful. No longer tending a fruitful, self-watering garden, Adam will now eat from his own fields by his own sweaty labor. He is thrown out of Eden "to work the ground from which he was taken." And the way to life is now barred (Genesis 3:14–24).

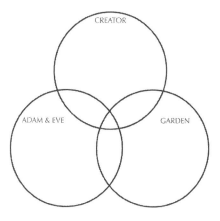

**Figure 4.** Creation and the Promise in Eden

This Venn diagram illustrates the development of our three themes through the eight promises of the framework summarized above. Each circle represents one of the themes—God, his people, his land—and each promise will contribute more understanding to each circle. So we see that in his hospitality, God the Creator provided a garden for us (Adam and Eve). He intended that we would cultivate it and craft it in his image. Our sin ruined that vision, and providing food became hard, painful labor.

## 2. The Promise to Abraham (Genesis 12–16)

Genesis 4–11 describes our ruined world. Granted, the description uses ancient forms and terms, but it is nonetheless a timeless description of pride, greed, lust, violence, and rebellion against the Creator. Judgment comes in the form of a flood, and only Noah is found righteous. The covenant is renewed to "be fruitful and multiply" (9:1), and once again God hospitably gives food to humanity. This time the animals and fish are included: "I give you everything" (9:3). Only one stipulation is made: respect the life—that is, the blood—and do not eat it (9:4).

The covenant with Noah and its rainbow sign refer explicitly to one of the most basic elements in human culture, namely the work of the farmer who cultivates the wilderness in order that it may bring forth food for human beings (Gen. 8:22). Here the interdependence of human beings and nature, and the dependence of both on the grace of God, are at their most manifest. God's promise that while earth remains seedtime and harvest shall not cease stands over the entire story of human culture. It is an assurance and an invitation to cherish and care for the earth and all that is in it, because God their creator cherishes and cares for them. And one of the counterthemes of the Old Testament is the perpetual tendency of Israel to forget the awesome and holy God who was the true author of prosperity, and to turn to the gods whose only function was to provide plenty of grain and oil and wine. Israel has to be reminded again and again by devastating disasters that the work of the farmer is only rightly undertaken when it is done as graceful acknowledgment of a gracious God. (Newbigin 1989, 194–195)

Still, yet again, men want to "make a name" for themselves, so they begin to build Babel or Babylon (11:4). And so we come to Genesis 12.

"Now the LORD said to Abram, 'Go . . .' " (12:1). This, of course, is a major hinge in the unfolding story—the second major promise. God chooses one in order to bless many. The specific promise of land is sealed with a blood covenant in chapter 15; the land from the Nile to the Euphrates is sworn to Abraham's descendants. Abraham is told it will take 400 years for the promise to be fulfilled. His descendants will be strangers and sojourners in a country that will enslave them. But then at last they will possess their land. In Genesis 13, famine drives Abram to Egypt, foreshadowing the events of Joseph and setting a pattern that follows the patriarchs as they wander in search of grain and grazing territory. For our purposes, it is important to note the "choosing" or "election" of Abram and his offspring. They will be as numerous as the stars! Somehow, their function or mission is to be a blessing to all peoples and families on the earth. As we are reminded in Deuteronomy, the Israelites were not chosen because they had privileged status with the Creator. They were chosen as his possession, to carry out his mission. In other words, systematic theology puts the doctrine of election in the wrong category; it belongs under missiology, not soteriology.

And so the narrative of the patriarchs ends in Genesis: Abraham, Isaac, Jacob/Israel, and finally Joseph—whose story involves (yet again) famine, food, and God's provision.

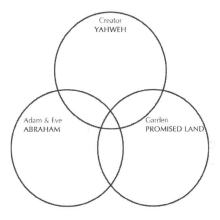

**Figure 5.** The Promise to Abraham

As figure 5 illustrates, our story has narrowed from the creation of the whole earth and all humanity to one man, Abraham, who is promised one land. Somehow, through Abraham and his "seed" (a collective noun that foreshadows both descendants and a descendant), the Creator, who is now known as Yahweh, will restore his vision of blessing to all people on the earth.

## 3. The Mosaic Covenant (Exodus 15–16, 31–35; Leviticus 19, 25; Deuteronomy 10:14–19)

When we turn to Exodus, we discover Moses and the great salvation story of Israel's liberation from Egypt. The Lord redeems for himself the people he had created from Abraham and Abraham's faith. Again, the link between food and worship is noted. The Passover takes place while the Israelites are eating. They are instructed to commemorate forever this great salvation event with a ceremonial meal. The Israelites plunder the Egyptians and begin their exodus being delivered through the waters of the parted sea. Pharaoh is once and for all defeated as his armies drown. And so we come to Exodus chapters 15–16.

Notice the salvation language in Moses' song of triumph. The Lord is motivated by his "steadfast love." He is "redeeming" his people, the people he "purchased." And he will "plant them" on the mountain that he has "made for [his] abode." In contrast to Pharaoh, the "chiefs of Edom," and all the gods and kings, "the LORD will *reign* for ever and ever" (Exodus 15:1–18, emphasis added).

Immediately the Lord's "saved" people begin to learn about walking with him, trusting him, and about what I will refer to as their "wilderness ethic." Their immediate need is water, but when they finally find some, it is bitter and undrinkable. God miraculously sweetens it for them, and through Moses, he tells them to "diligently listen to the voice of the LORD your God" (15:26).

In chapter 16, the Israelites are hungry! While only about a month has passed since Passover, they are beginning to look back on Egypt nostalgically—pining after the days "when [they] sat by the meat pots and ate bread to the full" (16:3). And so the Lord graciously promises to "rain bread from heaven for [them]" (16:4). The quails that come in the evening serve as meat, and manna in the mornings serve as bread—their daily bread. And it's meant to be "daily." The Israelites are not to worry about tomorrow; they are not to try to hoard either bread or meat. Instead they gather enough for their needs each day. (On the sixth day, they gather twice as much so they can rest on the Sabbath.) Once they had learned their lesson about hoarding—the manna spoiled when hoarded—the Israelites settled into their "wilderness ethic." As Exodus notes, "The people of Israel ate the manna forty years, till they came to a habitable land" (16:35). Their rhythm of life was one of trust and obedience. They gathered their daily bread, not being anxious for tomorrow, and trusted that their Redeemer would provide for them. They rested in faith on the Sabbath. This was the food ethic for a people with no settled land—an ethic for a sojourning people.

Next, Israel comes to Sinai in Exodus 19. There we note another explicit reference to kingdom. The Lord declares that "you shall be to me *a kingdom* of priests and a holy nation" (19:6, emphasis added). Though Israel pulls back in fear and becomes a kingdom *with* priests instead of a kingdom of priests, God's original desire is important to note. First, he claims that "all the earth" is his (19:5). God is the landlord; we are the tenants. We don't own any of it; he does. And on this earth that he owns, God wants his people to be priests in his image. Just as Adam was meant to work in God's image, so the Israelites were meant to mediate God's desires, policies, and wisdom to all the creatures of the earth. The Israelites' role was distinctive; they were "holy" or set apart for God's purposes *for the sake of others.*

Unfortunately, the Israelites respond in fear instead of in Abraham-like faith. Further instructions in God's wisdom begin to be added because of their transgressions (Sailhamer 1992, 51; Galatians 3:19). In particular, laws or instructions are given for a tabernacle. The tabernacle work looks back to the creation accounts, to the structure of God's universe and our earth, and to his good work in creation. The tabernacle also looks forward to the land and the temple, and even further to Jesus and his kingdom and to the new heavens and new earth and the good work to be done in and for them.

The work that will be required is set in contrast to the Israelites' slave labor in Egypt. There, the work was "forced," "ruthless" and "hard." It made their lives "bitter." Slave masters ruled over the Israelites "to afflict them with heavy burdens." The people built cities and did "all kinds of work in the field" (Exodus 1:11–14). This was in fulfillment of Adam's curse.

In contrast, the work on the tabernacle was to be good work, creating a sanctuary for the Lord among the people. This work would be guided by the Lord's Spirit (Exodus 31:2–4) and would be characterized by "ability and intelligence, with knowledge and all crafts-manship"—that is, by wisdom. Unfortunately, the first thing the people actually made was a golden calf. This transgression brought on more laws and instructions (Sailhamer 1992, 47). By Exodus 35, the people had repented and were eager to hear God's voice, so they begin bringing their offerings for the tabernacle. "All who were of a willing heart" and "whose heart moved them" brought the gold and silver plundered from the Egyptians (35:22–29). This was the opposite of the forced, slave labor in Egypt—and, for that matter, opposite of the work involved in making and worshipping an idol. This work was done from a willing heart, presented as an offering to the Lord, and performed by those with wisdom—that is, skill, knowledge, and ability given by God's Spirit. The Israelites did just as the Lord commanded, and at the end of Exodus, "the glory of the LORD filled the tabernacle" (40:34)—a tabernacle built on a pattern from God, a pattern for his people and the land he was giving them.

As the work in Eden was meant to be good work that would ensure plenty to eat and fellowship with God in the garden, so even after the fall in Genesis 3, God intended to bless his people with good work, not with slave labor in Egypt.

As the Israelites remained at Sinai, the instructions kept coming (Sailhamer 1992, 41), recorded for us in Leviticus. We need to note first Leviticus 19 and the issue of the poor and the foreigners who would be with the Israelites in the land, and then the year of Jubilee described in chapter 25.

God tells the Israelites that when they enter the land and it begins to be fruitful for them, they are not to harvest the fields clean. Rather, they are to leave some of the harvest at the margins of their fields for "the poor and for the sojourner" (Leviticus 19:10). They are to do justice, not favoring either the poor or the rich. Verse 18 sums it up with this command: "Love your neighbor as yourself." Then in verses 33–34, we read this specific instruction regarding those outside the chosen community—that is, sojourners or foreigners:

> "When a stranger *sojourns with you in your land*, you shall not do him wrong. You shall treat the stranger *who sojourns with you* as the native among you, and you shall love him as yourself,

for you were strangers in the land of Egypt: I am the LORD your God." (Emphasis added)

The command to love your neighbor envisioned fellow Israelites as its direct beneficiaries (19:17). The poor in particular were to receive justice and merciful consideration. There is, however, no consideration given in these instructions to the poor in surrounding nations, or to foreigners living in their own lands. But a foreigner who had joined the Israelites in the land and become an alien was to be treated as native-born. He was to be given the same kind of merciful consideration as the poor Israelite (19:10). The land, after all, was fruitful, flowing with milk and honey. It was to be used for livelihood and for food, but not just for the fortunate. The poor and the foreigners living among them were also to share in the hospitable provision of the land. But the land had to be respected and worked and kept as Adam had been commanded. It was to be worked as the tabernacle work had been done a generation before—in accordance with the Lord's instructions and by his Spirit. We should note that Israel and its land was not meant to be a source of provision to outsiders, but the Israelites and their land were meant to be the locus of provision for those in need in their midst. It was the alien living with them who had to be treated as native-born. And so we turn now to Jubilee and Leviticus 25.

"The land shall keep a Sabbath to the LORD" (Leviticus 25:2). The land is not like a mine, with natural resources that are to be removed like ore until all is taken. The land is not ore; it is an organism that needs regular renewal. "The land" is actually a complex web of relationships that include the land itself, the Israelites, their servants, their hired workers, their livestock, the aliens or foreigners living among them, and the wild animals (Leviticus 25:6–7). It is an entire kingdom of relationships. And according to Leviticus 25, every seven years it needed to rest from being worked and cultivated.

After "seven weeks of years" —that is, every fiftieth year—a Jubilee was to be declared (Leviticus 25:8–22). Note well the timing of the announcement of this special, once-in-a-generation super-Sabbath. It was to be announced on the Day of Atonement, accompanied by the proclamation of "liberty throughout the land" (25:10). The people's exodus salvation, their redemption from Pharaoh, their release from slavery in Egypt—all was to be both remembered and reenacted in their lives in the Lord's land. If the Exodus was a picture of how God's salvation begins (justification), then Jubilee is a picture of how God continues to correct, restore, and work out his salvation and atonement among his people in his land. In other words, it is a picture of sanctification.

The fundamental function of Jubilee for ancient Israel was to keep the land fairly distributed so the tribes, clans, and households could be sustained. Leviticus 25:10, 13, and 28 make it clear that the primary focus of Jubilee is the household—that multigenerational, traditional, socioeconomic unit that is foundational to all human societies. The text refers to "his property" or, in some translations, "family property." God's vision for his people is a society whose basic building block is an economically viable extended family. In that day, economically viable meant a landholding household. From the household is built the clan, and from the clans the tribe, and from the tribes the nation.

In addition, the households were to hold the land, work it, and keep it; but they did not *own* the land. "The land is mine," said the Lord (Leviticus 25:23). His people were his tenants. The extensive regulations about buying and selling land and redeeming it during Jubilee make clear that it was the use of the land that was being bought, sold, and redeemed—*not the land itself.* Further, the Israelites belonged to God as his "servants" (Leviticus 25:55). The high king owns the land of the kingdom, and his people are his servants, tenants on the land, stewarding it according to his laws and principles. If they will follow God's ways, then his creation vision will be restored; and as it was in Eden, so it will be in the land. "You shall eat your bread to the full and dwell in your land securely. I will give peace (*shalom*) in the land... I will walk among you and be your God, and you shall be my people" (Leviticus 26:5–12).

The tie to atonement and exodus is crucial. The overriding attitude enjoined on the people when they entered the land was gratitude. They had been aliens and strangers in Egypt. They had been landless and homeless. They had been redeemed from Pharaoh, given good work instead of slave labor. As a result of this grace, they were to treat one another and the slaves, servants, and aliens among them as the Lord had treated them. They had been forgiven of their sins; atonement had been made. So in Jubilee they could also forgive much and redeem much.

In the final part of the Torah, the scene shifts from the foot of Mount Sinai to the plains of Moab, just east of the Jordan River, with Jericho on the western horizon. As the suzerain treaty otherwise known as Deuteronomy is being spelled out, bringing the Torah to its close, we get a great summary of the issues pertinent to this study:

> "And now, Israel, what does the LORD your God require of you, but to fear the LORD your God, to walk in all his ways, to love him, to serve the LORD your God with all your heart and with all your soul, and to keep the commandments and statutes of the LORD, which I am commanding you today for your good? Behold, to the LORD your God belong heaven and the heaven of heavens, the earth with all that is in it. Yet the LORD set his heart in love on your fathers and chose their offspring after them, you above all peoples, as you are this day. Circumcise therefore the foreskin of your heart, and be no longer stubborn. For the LORD your God is God of gods and Lord of lords, the great, the mighty, and the awesome God, who is not partial and takes no bribe. He executes justice for the fatherless and the widow, and loves the sojourner, giving him food and clothing. Love the sojourner, therefore, for you were sojourners in the land of Egypt... and now the LORD your God has made you as numerous as the stars of heaven" (Deuteronomy 10:12–22)

From the land to the whole earth and heavens, it all belongs to the Lord—from one nation, Israel, which belongs to him, to everyone on the earth. All people on the whole earth belong to God. He has chosen his people, made in his own image, with the vision of them becoming a kingdom of priests for the sake of the whole world. God wants heart religion, not just rule keeping. "Circumcise your hearts!" he tells his people (Deuteronomy 10:16; 30:6). And so God's people would demonstrate his hospitable, loving ways by showing their grateful generosity to the orphan, the widow, and the alien in the land. The Israelites were to take the lessons of the wilderness and live them out in the land (that is, be the locus of *shalom*), following Yahweh's theological land ethic.

> The original wholeness (*shalom*) of creation is reestablished within the historical order. Underlying this picture are several relevant assumptions: that humans and land exist in a biotic unity before God, that their unity has identifiable moral dimensions (faithful action, truth, righteousness), that the moral restoration of God's people elicits God's gracious response in the form of agricultural productivity, and further... that human righteousness is the one condition that invites and even makes possible God's continued presence in the land. Those might be identified as the basic elements of the Bible's distinctively *theological* land ethic. (Davis 2009, 25–26)

This is the Torah's vision of relief and development. It is not a vision of people and wealth being shipped to distant lands. Rather, it is a vision of a people who provide relief for the poor and economic development for their brothers and for strangers who have chosen to join them. *Their life together in the land is R&D.* They are meant to be holy—distinct from the nations around them. Their economy is meant to be distinct.

Their treatment of the land is meant to be distinct. You might say that they and the land are Yahweh's R&D demonstration project for the whole earth.

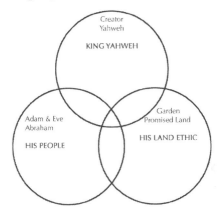

**Figure 6.** The Mosaic Covenant

## 4. The Early Prophets and the Promise to David. (2 Samuel 7; 1 Kings 21)

After the Torah closes, Israel crosses the Jordan and begins the occupation of the land. The people had been warned by Moses to remember their wilderness lessons, the "wilderness ethic," once they are at rest in the land. And they had been warned about kings. If they chose a king, he had to be "from among [their] brothers," a member of the covenant community who was under the authority of Yahweh and his Torah. An Israelite king must not multiply horses from Egypt (symbolizing military strength); he must not "acquire many wives" (symbolizing indulgence and pagan influence); and he must not have "excessive silver and gold," lest he and Israel become self-reliant, instead of reliant on Yahweh (Deuteronomy 17:14–20).

The trajectory of the Torah and the Early Prophets goes from landless to land to landless again. (By "Early Prophets," I am referring to those books sometimes labeled "Historical"—that is, Joshua, Judges, 1 and 2 Samuel, and 1 and 2 Kings. Following the Jewish tradition, I read them as prophetic works rather than as we would modern history.) The textual move in the Early Prophets is from wilderness sojourners to rest in the land to exiles from the land. Land won and land lost. By the end of Joshua, the land is conquered. While there is still much settling and work to be done (as there was in Eden), the author of Joshua is able to say unequivocally:

> "Thus the LORD gave to Israel all the land that he swore to give to their fathers. And they took possession of it, and they settled there. And the LORD gave them rest on every side just as he had sworn to their fathers. Not one of all their enemies had withstood them, for the LORD had given all their enemies into their hands. *Not one word of all the good promises that the* LORD *had made to the house of Israel had failed; all came to pass.*" (Joshua 21:43–45, emphasis added)

God has kept the promise of land he had made to Abraham. There is no unfulfilled promise that must be fulfilled at some future date. Yahweh's character is not at stake; he has kept his promise. Now the question is, will his people keep their promises?

Immediately in Judges, the people begin to disobey Yahweh their King. In chapter one, they fail to finish the conquest. By chapter two they are doing "what [is] evil in the sight of the LORD and [serving] the Baals"

(2:11–12). From Judges through 1 and 2 Samuel and 1 and 2 Kings, the process of losing the promised land is chronicled, until we come at last to 2 Kings 24:14–15: "[Nebuchadnezzar] carried away all Jerusalem… None remained, except the poorest people of the land. And he carried away [King] Jehoiachin to Babylon."

In the Early Prophets, we see God the King fulfill his promise to Abraham. Abraham's numerous descendants are no longer aliens and strangers without a home of their own; they are rescued slaves who have been given a place of refuge. They have been saved. Yahweh's economic provision for them is complete. While they still have work to do (as the first humans did in the garden), it is not slave labor as it was for the king of Egypt; it is worshipful work for the high King in his land.

In particular, it is to be a land of jubilee, a land of righteousness and justice. A land where the wisdom of the Torah is trustingly obeyed. A land and nation *unlike* the nations around them. A land and nation through whom the blessing of Abraham will flow to those surrounding nations. A land and nation to whom others from those nations can come for refuge, life, and wisdom. It is a land where possession does not bring entitlement, but responsibility and opportunity. The move from landless wilderness to landed nation does not decrease the need for care, for remembering, for trusting in Yahweh. Rather, it increases the need to trust and obey his wisdom, for the sake of his mission.

Unfortunately, by 1 Samuel 8 the people are already tiring of their distinctive mission. They want to be "like all the nations" and have a human king (8:5). In spite of Samuel's warnings, God tells the prophet to give the people what they want.

The story of Israel's kings is not incidental to the issue of economic provision and issues of R&D. As we see in the narrative, these kings do in fact become like the kings of other nations, ignoring Yahweh's ownership of the land and asserting their ownership instead. They lose the vision of kingship for the sake of the community, for the sake of implementing righteousness and justice, and substitute their own interests and glory.

Instead of regarding the land as a gracious provision for the people of God so there might be no poor among them, the kings view it as a "resource" for their own wasteful, careless, self-indulgence. Prophets begin to rise up precisely because there are such kings. Prophets rise up to remind the kings that there is a high King over them who owns the land of which they are merely stewards. Prophets remind the kings that their kingship is meant to be a blessing to the poorest Israelites and to the aliens and strangers among them. The land does not exist to support their self-centered lifestyle.

There are two paradigmatic episodes of king-versus-prophet confrontation in the Early Prophets that speak to our concern for economic provision and power. The first is centered around 2 Samuel 11, the episode of David and Bathsheba. The second is in 1 Kings 21, the story of Ahab, Jezebel, and Naboth's vineyard.

In 2 Samuel 7, God promises David a throne and a kingdom that will last forever. Further, God will raise up an offspring (seed) from David, and God himself will establish his kingdom:

"Moreover, the LORD declares to you that the LORD will make you a house. When your days are fulfilled and you lie down with your fathers, I will raise up your offspring after you, who shall come from your body, and I will establish his kingdom. He shall build a house for my name, and I will establish the throne of his kingdom forever. I will be to him a father, and he shall be to me a son... And your house and your kingdom shall be made sure forever before me. Your throne shall be established forever." (2 Samuel 7:11–16)

And yet, in 2 Samuel 11, we see the temptation that befalls kings. Others are out doing the king's work, fighting his battles; but David remains at leisure in Jerusalem. He steals Uriah's wife Bathsheba and impregnates her. Then David has others murder Uriah to cover up his sin—successfully, it would seem, until David is confronted by the prophet Nathan. Nathan tells a tale of a lamb stolen from a poor man by a rich man. When David reacts with righteous indignation, Nathan confronts him: "You are the man!" (12:7). To his credit, David repents, but there are consequences to his actions—including the death of Bathsheba's child. David didn't just sin against Bathsheba and Uriah; he "utterly scorned the LORD" (12:14).

Kings are tempted to think of themselves as owners. Kings are tempted to grasp and control whatever they want. Kings are tempted to use their positions of power for personal advantage.

Prophets remind the kings that they are stewards. Prophets remind them that their land and power are gifts to be received. Prophets remind kings that their influence, wealth, and power are to be used for the community's advantage (2 Samuel 8:15).

The key issues, then, are ownership versus stewardship, grasping control versus receiving a gift, and personal advantage versus community advantage.

David's son Solomon was the tipping point. His reign sealed the doom of the land, though it took some time to play out. In 1 Kings 4, we read that, "Judah and Israel were as many as the sand by the sea. They ate and drank and were happy" (4:20). Aren't these the goals of relief and development?

The temple is built, and in Solomon's remarkable prayer of dedication, we catch a vision of Yahweh's people in the land, a land wrapped around Jerusalem and the temple, as the locus of blessing for the nations around Israel:

> "Likewise, when a foreigner, who is not of your people Israel, comes from a far country for your name's sake (for they shall hear of your great name and your mighty hand, and of your outstretched arm), when he comes and prays toward this house, hear in heaven your dwelling place and do according to all for which the foreigner calls to you, in order that all the peoples of the earth may know your name and fear you, as do your people Israel, and that they may know that this house that I have built is called by your name." (1 Kings 8:41–43)

The Lord promises in 1 Kings 9:4 that if Solomon will walk in trusting obedience, then the promise to David will be extended through Solomon, and his throne will be established forever. But Solomon does not walk in obedience. In chapter 10, the queen of Sheba visits Solomon. She seems to understand the Lord's intention for kings better than Solomon does:

> "Blessed be the LORD your God, who has delighted in you and set you on the throne of Israel! Because the LORD loved Israel forever, he has made you king, *that you may execute justice and righteousness*." (1 Kings 10:9, emphasis added)

After the account of the queen of Sheba's visit, 1 Kings 10 gives a detailed description of all that Solomon has amassed: excessive amounts of gold and silver (10:14–22); huge numbers of chariots and horses, imported from Egypt (10:26–29); a multitude of pagan wives (11:1–8). All this he collected for himself in direct disobedience to the warnings of the Torah (see Deuteronomy 17:14–20) and of Samuel (see 1 Samuel 8:10–18). As for the foreigners, instead of treating them hospitably as if they were fellow Israelites, Solomon drafted them into forced slave labor (1 Kings 9:15). Thus "Solomon creates a situation not unlike that of Pharaoh" (Brueggemann 1977, 86). The necessary prophet, Ahijah, rises up to announce that God is "about to tear the kingdom from the hand of Solomon" (11:31). After Solomon's death, the kingdom is divided, and so begins the long, tragic history of the divided kingdoms of Israel and Judah.

Thus David's failure with covetousness was made fully manifest in his son Solomon. But there is another paradigmatic episode in the Early Prophets: that of Ahab and Jezebel, a wicked king and queen. Here we see an even clearer contrast between the distinctive economics of Yahweh's land and pagan (specifically, Canaanite) ideas about money, wealth, and power.

In 1 Kings 21, King Ahab sees another man's vineyard and wants it for himself. He apparently wants to take Naboth's vineyard and replace it with a vegetable garden. Naboth speaks just one line in 21:3, which sums up the Torah's teaching about the land and its use: "The LORD forbid that I should give you the inheritance of my fathers." Naboth intuitively understands the concept of stewardship. The Lord had forbidden the selling of land, even when it's the king's money being offered. Naboth's land was held in trust by his family, in stewardship for the Lord. It was meant to be the economic provision for his family and clan. He was obligated to *not* sell it, but rather to work it and keep it for the sake of his people.

Rebuffed, Ahab is despondent and takes to pouting. But not Jezebel. She asks her husband, "Do you now govern Israel?" (21:7). Then Jezebel has Naboth murdered, and Ahab seizes the vineyard "to take possession of it" (21:16)—ownership instead of stewardship.

The prophet Elijah confronts Ahab. "You have sold yourself to do what is evil in the sight of the LORD. Behold, I will bring disaster upon you" (1 Kings 21:20–21). The writer sums up the situation as follows: "There was none who sold himself to do what was evil in the sight of the LORD like Ahab, whom Jezebel his wife incited" (21:25). A king of Israel, who was supposed to avoid multiplying wives, pagan wives, and who was supposed to copy the Torah and read it all his life, instead had implemented the Canaanite golden rule: He who has the gold makes the rules.

In spite of the prophets (including the writing prophets who we will explore below), the kings of the land lose the land. They were the people entrusted with the wealth and power to shape the society of God's people in God's way. They had the authority, the influence, and the means to implement the distinctive economics of the Exodus and of the Jubilee. But they succumbed to the ways of the world, to Canaanite and Egyptian economic "theory," and they scorned the high King of Israel and his ways. And so, Israel loses the land:

> Unlike all neighbors, the king [of Israel] is subjected to the Torah... Power is put in the service of a special faith and a peculiar vision. Such a view of kingship asserts a dominant conviction of the Bible that is against the wisdom of the world... The way to keep the land and power over it is to turn attention from land to Torah. By implication the way to lose land is to be anxious about it to the neglect of Torah...
>
> The Torah tells the king he is a brother of the other brothers and sisters... Land is not, if viewed as a gift, for self-security but for the brother and sister. (Brueggemann 1977, 78)

This land loss was stunning. The land had been promised and delivered by God. Grace had been given and received. Now it was all lost. Heirs became exiles. Promised land, it turns out, can be lost. Keeping hold of the land and obeying Yahweh are so intertwined that they cannot be separated.

So what of modern-day Canaanite economics or Torah economics? What about Jezebel-like ideas of land ownership and grasping possession versus Naboth's covenant with the Lord to steward the land as a gift? What of "modern kings" who have all the wealth, the political clout, the power to shape societies, laws, and economies? In particular, what of the wealth, possessions, power, influence, and "kingship" exercised by members of the people of God, members of the body of Christ?

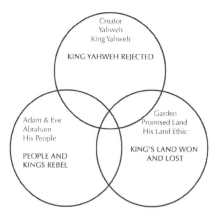

**Figure 7.** The Early Prophets and the Promise to David

Our diagram documents a tragedy. A vision for humanity is lost in the Garden of Eden. God in his grace promises to Abraham that he will restore that vision. King Yahweh saves a people, a kingdom of priests, and teaches them how to join in his mission to restore the whole earth. But his people—and especially their powerful leaders—rebel. Once again, paradise is lost.

## 5. The Latter Prophets and the Promised Day of the Lord (Amos, Hosea, Micah, Jeremiah, and Isaiah)

While the Early Prophets provide the story of the period from conquest to exile, the Latter Prophets provide the prophetic commentary of what went wrong, and they begin to point beyond land loss to a restoration— a restoration that will extend beyond Israel to include the nations. This Day of the Lord will bring provision and blessing and *shalom* to the whole world, in final consummation of Yahweh's promise to Abraham. There is a large amount of material to cover, so we start with the minor prophets of Amos, Hosea, and Micah as they address the economics of rebellion and judgment. Then we will consider the pre-Assyrian major prophet Isaiah and the prophet of the Babylonian exile, Jeremiah.

Amos wastes no time. After announcing God's displeasure with Israel's neighbors, and with Israel and Judah as well, he gets down to specifics with Israel. Amos 4:1–3:

> "Hear this word, you cows of Bashan, who are on the mountain of Samaria, who oppress the poor, who crush the needy, who say to your husbands, 'Bring, that we may drink!' The LORD God has sworn by his holiness that, behold, the days are coming upon you, when they shall take you away with hooks, even the last of you with fishhooks. And you shall go out through the breaches, each one straight ahead; and you shall be cast out into Harmon," declares the LORD.

And 5:12:

For I know how many are your transgressions and how great are your sins—you who afflict the righteous, who take a bribe, and turn aside the needy in the gate.

And 6:1–7:

"Woe to those who are at ease in Zion, and to those who feel secure on the mountain of Samaria, the notable men of the first of the nations, to whom the house of Israel comes! Pass over to Calneh, and see, and from there go to Hamath the great; then go down to Gath of the Philistines. Are you better than these kingdoms? Or is their territory greater than your territory, O you who put far away the day of disaster and bring near the seat of violence? Woe to those who lie on beds of ivory and stretch themselves out on their couches, and eat lambs from the flock and calves from the midst of the stall, who sing idle songs to the sound of the harp and like David invent for themselves instruments of music, who drink wine in bowls and anoint themselves with the finest oils, but are not grieved over the ruin of Joseph! Therefore they shall now be the first of those who go into exile, and the revelry of those who stretch themselves out shall pass away."

Israel's worship and its economic policies are intertwined. The Lord wants something other than their ritualistic worship:

"I hate, I despise your feasts, and I take no delight in your solemn assemblies. Even though you offer me your burnt offerings and grain offerings, I will not accept them; and the peace offerings of your fattened animals, I will not look upon them. Take away from me the noise of your songs; to the melody of your harps I will not listen. But let justice roll down like waters, and righteousness like an ever-flowing stream. Did you bring to me sacrifices and offerings during the forty years in the wilderness, O house of Israel? You shall take up Sikkuth your king, and Kiyyun your star-god— your images that you made for yourselves, and I will send you into exile beyond Damascus," says the LORD, whose name is the God of hosts. (Amos 5:21–27)

Israel has failed to become a distinctive people whose life is characterized by "righteousness and justice" by obedience to a wilderness ethic of sharing instead of hoarding. Yet even this word of judgment ends with a vision of restoration:

"I will restore the fortunes of my people Israel, and they shall rebuild the ruined cities and inhabit them; they shall plant vineyards and drink their wine, and they shall make gardens and eat their fruit. I will plant them on their land, and they shall never again be uprooted out of the land that I have given them," says the LORD your God. (Amos 9:14–15)

The prophet Hosea is famous for his marriage to the prostitute Gomer. His prophecy states in no uncertain terms coming doom for the northern kingdom Israel. Important for our concerns is the prophet's insistence that the prostitute Israel has forgotten the economic provision of her husband the Lord:

> "For their mother has played the whore; she who conceived them has acted shamefully. For she said, 'I will go after my lovers, who give me my bread and my water, my wool and my flax, my oil and my drink.' Therefore I will hedge up her way with thorns, and I will build a wall against her, so that she cannot find her paths. She shall pursue her lovers but not overtake them, and she shall seek them but shall not find them. Then she shall say, 'I will go and return to my first husband, for it was better for me then than now.' And she did not know that it was I who gave her the grain, the wine, and the oil, and who lavished on her silver and gold, which they used for Baal. Therefore I will take back my grain in its time, and my wine in its season, and I will take away my wool and my flax, which were to cover her nakedness. Now I will uncover her lewdness in the sight of her lovers, and no one shall rescue her out of my hand." (Hosea 2:5–10)

The land and its provision belong to the Lord, not to any other king or "lover." In chapter three, Hosea buys Gomer back and redeems her. Similarly, the Lord looks forward to that distant day when he will redeem his people:

> Afterward the children of Israel shall return and seek the LORD their God, and David their king, and they shall come in fear to the LORD and to his goodness in the latter days. (Hosea 3:5)

But in the meantime, "the LORD has a controversy with the inhabitants of the land":

> There is no faithfulness or steadfast love, and no knowledge of God in the land; there is swearing, lying, murder, stealing, and committing adultery; they break all bounds, and bloodshed follows bloodshed. Therefore the land mourns, and all who dwell in it languish, and also the beasts of the field and the birds of the heavens, and even the fish of the sea are taken away. (Hosea 4:1–3)

The Israelites' lack of covenant faithfulness and their lack of trusting obedience have affected the nonhuman inhabitants of Israel; even the land itself mourns. This link between the people's ethical distinctiveness—or the lack of it—and the condition of the land and its provision for them is important. The connection shouldn't surprise us, since "like Adam they transgressed the covenant" (Hosea 6:7). Just as Adam's disobedience and lack of trust affected all creation, now the land and its economy suffer because of Israel's disobedience. Even though "Israel is a luxuriant vine that yields its fruit" (10:1), the more its people prosper, the more they build altars of false worship. Now the Lord "will break down their altars" (10:2).

> In fact, the Lord openly mocks their political and economic arrangements:
>
> Where now is your king, to save you in all your cities? Where are all your rulers—those of whom you said, "Give me a king and princes"? I gave you a king in my anger, and I took him away in my wrath. (Hosea 13:10–11)

From Hosea we turn to Micah and his pronouncement of doom on both the northern and southern kingdoms of Israel and Judah. Chapter one introduces this sure and certain judgment, explaining why it is coming:

> Woe to those who devise wickedness and work evil on their beds! When the morning dawns, they perform it, because it is in the power of their hand. They covet fields and seize them, and houses, and take them away; they oppress a man and his house, a man and his inheritance. Therefore thus says the LORD: behold, against this family I am devising disaster, from which you cannot remove your necks, and you shall not walk haughtily, for it will be a time of disaster. (Micah 2:1–3)

Their leaders have become corrupt, and those who should have led in justice now "hate the good and love the evil" (3:1–2). And so disaster is coming.

But first comes a vision of "the latter days." In Micah 4 and 5, we see the distant day when "the mountain of the house of the LORD shall be established" and "peoples shall flow to it, and many nations shall come" to learn the Lord's ways and to walk in his paths (4:1). War will pass away (4:3), and every man will have shelter and food (4:4). A remnant will enter into the Lord's kingdom, and from little Bethlehem will come the Lord's ruler, who "shall be their peace" (5:2–5). Before that day comes, however, the Lord has a case to make against his people before the "jury" of the land:

> Hear what the LORD says: Arise, plead your case before the mountains, and let the hills hear your voice. Hear, you mountains, the indictment of

the LORD, and you enduring foundations of the earth, for the LORD has an indictment against his people, and he will contend with Israel. "O my people, what have I done to you? How have I wearied you? Answer me! For I brought you up from the land of Egypt and redeemed you from the house of slavery, and I sent before you Moses, Aaron, and Miriam. O my people, remember what Balak king of Moab devised, and what Balaam the son of Beor answered him, and what happened from Shittim to Gilgal, that you may know the righteous acts of the LORD." (Micah 6:1–5)

God had saved Israel from Egypt. Now the land itself bears witness that God has done nothing but protect and provide for his people ever since. In return, did he desire their temple, their sacrifices, their burnt offerings? If not, what did he want from them?

"He has told you, O man, what is good; and what does the LORD require of you but to do justice, and to love kindness, and to walk humbly with your God?" (Micah 6:8)

And how had the people behaved in return?

The voice of the LORD cries to the city—and it is sound wisdom to fear your name: "Hear of the rod and of him who appointed it! Can I forget any longer the treasures of wickedness in the house of the wicked, and the scant measure that is accursed? Shall I acquit the man with wicked scales and with a bag of deceitful weights? Your rich men are full of violence; your inhabitants speak lies, and their tongue is deceitful in their mouth. Therefore I strike you with a grievous blow, making you desolate because of your sins. You shall eat, but not be satisfied, and there shall be hunger within you; you shall put away, but not preserve, and what you preserve I will give to the sword. You shall sow, but not reap; you shall tread olives, but not anoint yourselves with oil; you shall tread grapes, but not drink wine." (Micah 6:9–15)

Their behavior in the land will now cost them the land. Yet there is hope. There will be a remnant. There is a far-off future day, as described in Micah 7. God will show his "steadfast love to Abraham" (7:20). But for now, both of the divided kingdoms have a judgment coming.

Next, we turn to the book of Isaiah. The prophet Isaiah pronounces the coming doom, the sure judgment, and the loss of the land. At the same time, the book offers a sweeping vision of a coming day when all nations (remember God's promise to Abraham?) will stream into the land. Jerusalem, or Zion, will be seen as the place of peace and justice. The nations will come, compelled not by force but by the persuasive example of God's people in Zion:

O Lord, you are my God; I will exalt you; I will praise your name, for you have done wonderful things, plans formed of old, faithful and sure. For you have made the city a heap, the fortified city a ruin; the foreigners' palace is a city no more; it will never be rebuilt. Therefore strong peoples will glorify you; cities of ruthless nations will fear you. For you have been a stronghold to the poor, a stronghold to the needy in his distress, a shelter from the storm and a shade from the heat; for the breath of the ruthless is like a storm against a wall, like heat in a dry place. You subdue the noise of the foreigners; as heat by the shade of a cloud, so the song of the ruthless is put down. On this mountain the LORD of hosts will make for all peoples a feast of rich food, a feast of well-aged wine, of rich food full of marrow, of aged wine well refined. And he will swallow up on this mountain the covering that is cast over all peoples, the veil that is spread over all nations. He will swallow up death forever; and the Lord GOD will wipe away tears from all faces, and the reproach of his people he will take away from all the earth, for the LORD has spoken. It will be said on that day, "Behold, this is our God; we have waited for him, that he might save us. This is the LORD; we have waited for him; let us be glad and rejoice in his salvation." (Isaiah 25:1–9)

Isaiah's vision of the people's life together is compelling. He does not simply see religious practice and ritual. He sees a vision of a people who demonstrate an altogether different way to live:

"Cry aloud; do not hold back; lift up your voice like a trumpet; declare to my people their transgression, to the house of Jacob their sins. Yet they seek me daily and delight to know my ways, as if they were a nation that did righteousness and did not forsake the judgment of their God; they ask of me righteous judgments; they delight to draw near to God. 'Why have we fasted, and you see it not? Why have we humbled ourselves, and you take no knowledge of it?' Behold, in the day of your fast you seek your own pleasure, and oppress all your workers. Behold, you fast only to quarrel and to fight and to hit with a wicked fist. Fasting like yours this day will not make your voice to be heard on high. Is such the fast that I choose, a day for a person to humble himself? Is it to bow down his head like a reed, and to spread sackcloth and ashes under him? Will you call this a fast, and a day acceptable to the LORD? Is not this the fast that I choose: to loose the bonds of wickedness, to undo the straps of the yoke, to let the oppressed go free, and to break every yoke? Is it not to share your bread with the hungry and bring the homeless poor into your house; when you see the naked, to cover him, and not to hide yourself from your own flesh? Then shall your light break forth like the dawn, and your healing shall spring up speedily; your righteousness shall go before you; the glory of the LORD shall be your rear guard. Then you shall call, and the LORD will answer; you shall cry, and he will say, 'Here I am.' If you take away the yoke from your midst, the pointing of the finger, and speaking wickedness, if you pour yourself out for the hungry and satisfy the desire of the afflicted, then shall your light rise in the darkness and your gloom be as the noonday. And the LORD will guide you continually and satisfy your desire in scorched places and make your bones strong; and you shall be like a watered garden, like a spring of water, whose waters do not fail. And your ancient ruins shall be rebuilt; you shall raise up the foundations of many generations; you shall be called the repairer of the breach, the restorer of streets to dwell in." (Isaiah 58:1–12)

The sixtieth chapter of Isaiah offers a breathtaking vision of the diversity of peoples and nations who "shall come to your light" (v.3), that is, the light of God's people. God will "beautify the place of [his] sanctuary" and "make the place of [his] feet glorious" (60:13). In fact, God will also do the following:

Instead of bronze I will bring gold, and instead of iron I will bring silver; instead of wood, bronze, instead of stones, iron. I will make your overseers peace and your taskmasters righteousness. Violence shall no more be heard in your land, devastation or destruction within your borders; you shall call your walls Salvation, and your gates Praise. (Isaiah 60:17–18)

The vision continues until the end of chapter 62:

And they shall be called The Holy People, The Redeemed of the LORD; and you shall be called Sought Out, A City Not Forsaken. (Isaiah 62:12)

In the midst of this vision we hear this famous passage:

The Spirit of the Lord GOD is upon me, because the LORD has anointed me to bring good news to the poor; he has sent me to bind up the broken-hearted, to proclaim liberty to the captives, and the opening of the prison to those who are bound; to proclaim the year of the LORD's favor, and the day of vengeance of our God; to comfort all who mourn." (Isaiah 61:1–2a)

It should not be lost on us that the Lord Jesus uses this passage—and the surrounding context by implication—to announce the beginning of his own ministry, his purpose in coming among us. As we will see later, Jesus and his movement are the fulfillment of Isaiah's vision.

Writing over one hundred years after Isaiah, the reluctant prophet Jeremiah has much to say about our themes of God, his people, and his land. Walter Brueggemann says of Jeremiah, "In the Old Testament he is the poet of the land par excellence" (Brueggemann 1977, 107). And Jeremiah's message is hard for Israel (and us?) to hear: "His message to Israel, which thought it was ultimately secure and at home, is the coming ultimate homelessness" (108):

Thus says the LORD: "Behold, a people is coming from the north country, a great nation is stirring from the farthest parts of the earth. They lay hold on bow and javelin; they are cruel and have no mercy; the sound of them is like the roaring sea; they ride on horses, set in array as a man for battle, against you, O daughter of Zion!" (Jeremiah 6:22–23)

Further, Jeremiah announces something radically new for God's people. The old covenant has been broken. God's judgment is certain, and he has a new vision for his people. Jeremiah 24 uses the imagery of a basket of good figs and a basket of bad figs to explain this new vision:

> Then the word of the LORD came to me: "Thus says the LORD, the God of Israel: Like these good figs, so I will regard as good the exiles from Judah, whom I have sent away from this place to the land of the Chaldeans. I will set my eyes on them for good, and I will bring them back to this land. I will build them up, and not tear them down; I will plant them, and not pluck them up. I will give them a heart to know that I am the LORD, and they shall be my people and I will be their God, for they shall return to me with their whole heart. But thus says the LORD: Like the bad figs that are so bad they cannot be eaten, so will I treat Zedekiah the king of Judah, his officials, the remnant of Jerusalem who remain in this land, and those who dwell in the land of Egypt. I will make them a horror to all the kingdoms of the earth, to be a reproach, a byword, a taunt, and a curse in all the places where I shall drive them. And I will send sword, famine, and pestilence upon them, until they shall be utterly destroyed from the land that I gave to them and their fathers." (Jeremiah 24:4–10)

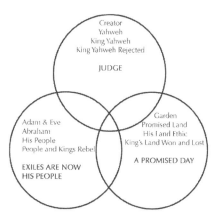

**Figure 8.** The Latter Prophets and the Promised Day of the Lord

Those who have a heart for God the righteous Judge will now be the exiles. God is with the exiles, not with those who cling to the old failed covenant and the old land. God's people are once again entering the wilderness, where they will travel with him. And as they travel, they will become the fulfillment of the Abrahamic promise to bless the nations:

> "Thus says the LORD of hosts, the God of Israel, to all the exiles whom I have sent into exile from Jerusalem to Babylon: Build houses and live in them; plant gardens and eat their produce. Take wives and have sons and daughters; take wives for your sons, and give your daughters in marriage, that they may bear sons and daughters; multiply there, and do not decrease. *But seek the welfare of the city where I have sent you into exile, and pray to the* LORD *on its behalf, for in its welfare you will find your welfare.* For thus says the LORD of hosts, the God of Israel: Do not let your prophets and your diviners who are

among you deceive you, and do not listen to the dreams that they dream, for it is a lie that they are prophesying to you in my name; I did not send them, declares the LORD. For thus says the LORD: When seventy years are completed for Babylon, I will visit you, and I will fulfill to you my promise and bring you back to this place. For I know the plans I have for you, declares the LORD, plans for welfare and not for evil, to give you a future and a hope." (Jeremiah 29:4–11, emphasis added)

"Seek the welfare" of sinful, conquering, pagan Babylon! For in its peace, God's people will find peace. And though the Babylonian exile will last only seventy years, the people should not expect that their return will mean a return to business as usual. The old land covenant is broken; it will not be renewed (Jeremiah 45:4). Instead, something new is coming:

"Behold, the days are coming, declares the LORD, when I will make a new covenant with the house of Israel and the house of Judah, not like the covenant that I made with their fathers on the day when I took them by the hand to bring them out of the land of Egypt, my covenant that they broke, though I was their husband, declares the LORD. For this is the covenant that I will make with the house of Israel after those days, declares the LORD: I will put my law within them, and I will write it on their hearts. And I will be their God, and they shall be my people. And no longer shall each one teach his neighbor and each his brother, saying, 'Know the LORD,' for they shall all know me, from the least of them to the greatest, declares the LORD. For I will forgive their iniquity, and I will remember their sin no more." (Jeremiah 31:31–34)

And though the old Mosaic covenant of the promised land is gone, a better promise will still be kept:

"Behold, the days are coming, declares the LORD, when I will fulfill the promise I made to the house of Israel and the house of Judah. In those days and at that time I will cause a righteous Branch to spring up for David, and he shall execute justice and righteousness in the land." (Jeremiah 33:14–15)

The word of the LORD came to Jeremiah: "Thus says the LORD: If you can break my covenant with the day and my covenant with the night, so that day and night will not come at their appointed time, then also my covenant with David my servant may be broken, so that he shall not have a son to reign on his throne, and my covenant with the Levitical priests my ministers." (Jeremiah 33:19–21)

"Thus says the LORD: If I have not established my covenant with day and night and the fixed order of heaven and earth, then I will reject the offspring of Jacob and David my servant and will not choose one of his offspring to rule over the offspring of Abraham, Isaac, and Jacob. For I will restore their fortunes and will have mercy on them." (Jeremiah 33:25–26)

We now turn to the fulfillment of that promise.

# The Messiah, His Messengers, and His Movement (The New Testament)

We seem to lose one circle of our Venn diagram when we turn the page from Malachi to Matthew: how does the land figure into the New Testament? We have been working on the premise that land is one of the big three themes of our Bible and our faith. In the New Testament, we get even more revelation about the first two themes: God and the revealed mystery of his people. But the third theme of land seems to disappear.

Hope is no longer held out to God's people for a geographical relocation or return. The new "Israel," composed of Jew and Gentile (Romans 11:13–24), does not begin a pilgrimage back to the Middle East from the far-flung cities of the Roman Empire. Roman Christians do not pack up and move back to the land after they are grafted into the people of God.

Jesus warned his own people again and again of the futility of hanging on to the land by violence. He predicted, in no uncertain terms, the destruction of the land's ultimate symbols—Jerusalem and its temple (see, for instance, Luke 19:41–44). So is the New Testament done with the land?

No. The land and its implications are everywhere in the teachings of Christ and his apostles. I grew up learning a theology that took all land and kingdom references in the New Testament to be referring to the afterlife—that is, to heaven. When you come across references to "the kingdom of heaven" (Matthew 11:11), our "inheritance" (Ephesians 5:5), "rest" (Hebrews 4:1), "Mount Zion" and "the heavenly Jerusalem"

(Hebrews 12:22), then you are seeing the land spiritualized into a description of the heavenly afterlife. The old land language and expectations no longer apply to the physical world; instead they are foreshadows of unseen heavenly realities—the eternal, afterlife salvation of our souls.

This particular form of spiritualizing fails to take seriously Jesus' announcement in Luke 4: "I must preach the good news of the kingdom of God to the other towns as well; for I was sent for this purpose" (Luke 4:43). Or when he announced to the Pharisees, "The kingdom of God is not coming in ways that can be observed, nor will they say, 'Look, here it is!' or 'There!' for behold, the kingdom of God is in the midst of you" (Luke 17:20–21). When Jesus is present, the kingdom is present. True, the kingdom is not yet in its fullest consummation. But it has begun. It is really here, and not to be relegated solely to the afterlife.

The dispensationalist view sees the geographical promise of land as simply being put on hold for a while—namely, during the church age. This view expects this promise to be fulfilled to ethnic Jews at some point in the future, either just before the eschaton or just after in the millennium. This view is driven primarily by an understanding of the Abrahamic covenant as including an unconditional promise of unending, geographically specific land ownership. This view cannot be sustained by a fair reading of the Early and Latter Prophets, who clearly thought that God had in fact fulfilled his promise of land to the Israelites (see, for example, Joshua 21:43–45). But Israel broke the land covenant and justifiably lost their inheritance. There is no longer a

FRAMEWORK FOR A CHURCH-BASED THEOLOGY OF RELIEF AND DEVELOPMENT

land promise left to fulfill. God's integrity is not at stake. He kept his promise. Israel did not keep theirs. Dispensationalism is a view driven by impoverished hermeneutics and inadequate biblical theology. We can do better. Gary Burge puts it this way:

> At no point do the earliest Christians view the Holy Land as a locus of divine activity to which the people of the Roman empire must be drawn. They do not promote the Holy Land either for the Jew or for the Christian as a vital aspect of faith. No diaspora Jew or pagan Roman is converted and then reminded of the importance of the Holy Land. The early Christians possessed no territorial theology. Early Christian preaching is utterly *uninterested* in a Jewish eschatology devoted to the restoration of the land. The kingdom of Christ began in Judea and is historically anchored there but it is not tethered to a political realization of that kingdom in the Holy Land. Echoing the message of the Gospels, the praxis of the Church betrays it theological commitments: Christians will find in *Christ* what Judaism had sought in the land. (Burge 2010, 59)

There are two words that do better justice to the New Testament's teaching about the land: fulfillment and extension.

## 6. Fulfillment in Christ

Jesus came not to abolish the Law, but to fulfill it (Matthew 5:17). By this statement, he did not mean the laws contained in the Law, but the prophetic message of the Torah as a text. He was the *autobasilea*—the kingdom-in-himself. Wherever he was, there was the kingdom. Throughout the Gospels, Jesus inaugurated the long-awaited kingdom-in-the-land. He made clear that this kingdom was not yet consummated. But he was equally clear that it had already begun (Matthew 12:28). Jesus was the fulfillment of the land promise. He was "the true vine" (John 15:1), not just for ethnic Israel in a specific and limited geographical location.

The Gospel writer Luke wasted no time in making this land-king-kingdom connection. The opening chapter of his Gospel is about kings ("the days of Herod") and kingdoms ("king of Judea"). It is about the temple and temple service, about the "house of David." Mary's Magnificat (Luke 1:46–55) invokes prophetic language about the downfall of thrones and the rich, about new economic arrangements. It reminds us of the land promise, "to Abraham and to his offspring forever" (1:55). Perhaps most remarkable is Jesus' presentation in the temple "according to the Law of Moses" (2:22)—at which point, the devout Simeon, righteously waiting for the "consolation of Israel" (2:25), scoops up the infant Jesus and announces:

> "Lord, now you are letting your servant depart in peace, according to your word; for my eyes have seen your salvation that you have prepared in the presence of all peoples, a light for revelation to the Gentiles, and for glory to your people Israel." (Luke 2:29–32)

All that has been hoped for—full return from exile, full possession of the land, full freedom from pagan domination and conquest (that is, salvation)—is now fulfilled in this Jesus. It's as if Simeon himself personifies the Law and the Prophets and announces, "Here is our fulfillment." Look no more to the promised land, but to the Promised One.

Luke then turns to Jesus' own wilderness experience (Luke 4:1–13), a parallel to ancient Israel as they sojourned in preparation for the promised land. Next, Jesus launches his ministry—his kingdom enterprise—with the quote from Isaiah 61:1–2 we mentioned earlier.

> And he came to Nazareth, where he had been brought up. And as was his custom, he went to the synagogue on the Sabbath day, and he stood up to read. And the scroll of the prophet Isaiah was given to him. He unrolled the scroll and found the place where it was written, "The Spirit of the Lord is upon me, because he has anointed me to proclaim good news to the poor. He has sent me to proclaim liberty to the captives and recovering of sight to the blind, to set at liberty those who are oppressed, to proclaim the year of the Lord's favor." And he rolled up the scroll and gave it back to the attendant and sat down. And the eyes of all in the synagogue were fixed on him. And he began to say to them, "Today this Scripture has been fulfilled in your hearing." (Luke 4:16–21)

The land has become Jesus. He is the fulfillment of the land hope, lost in disobedience and exile, now restored. The land hope is not fulfilled geographically, but personally. Wherever Jesus goes, he demonstrates the blessings of the land—provision, food, deliverance, peace—all of which can now be found wherever he is!

The "meek... shall inherit the earth," according to Jesus (Matthew 5:5)—that is, the meek who follow him. There's a new land arrangement, just as Mary sang—one in which it's not the powerful kings of the earth who control the land but "those of humble estate" (Luke 1:52) who follow Jesus. There is food and provision "in Christ." He feeds the five thousand (Luke 9:10–17) and the four thousand (Matthew 15:32–39). Many have noted Jesus' extensive ministry and teaching around banquet tables; these scenes represent Isaiah 25 inaugurated. "But when you give a feast, invite the poor, the crippled, the lame, the blind," Jesus declares in Luke 14:12–24. Jesus heals (Luke 5:12–26). He exorcises (Luke 6:17–19). A realm is being made in which to experience blessing and *shalom*.

In recapitulation and fulfillment of the slain Passover lamb (Exodus 12:1–32), the parting of the sea of death (Exodus 14:1–31), and the wilderness ethic (Exodus 16:31–36) to prepare for a promised land (Deuteronomy 34:1–8), we now have the following in Christ: the cross (1 Corinthians 5:7), the resurrection (1 Corinthians 15:20–26), a pilgrim church (1 Peter 2:9–12), and the blessed hope of a new earth (Revelation 21:1–8).

The wilderness and land ethic taught in the Scriptures continues throughout the Gospels. In Jesus' kingdom, there is to be no hoarding; only a fool builds bigger barns (Luke 12:13–21). The manna still rots if hoarded; moth and rust destroy and thieves break in and steal (Luke 12:32–34). The rich who ignore the poor are in danger of Gehenna and its judgment (Luke 16:19–31). In fact, they are well on their way to becoming goats and suffering a horrible fate at the last judgment (Matthew 25:31–46). Instead of selfishness, there is generosity. "Sell your possessions, and give to the needy" (Luke 12:33). "Give, and it will be given to you" (Luke 6:38). Money is a tool, a dangerous tool, meant to be used for the kingdom. "Make friends for yourselves by means of unrighteous wealth, so that when it fails they may receive you into the eternal dwellings" (Luke 16:9).

The clear teaching of stewardship continues as well. The land did not belong to Israel. Neither does the wealth that is entrusted to the followers of Jesus. "A nobleman went into a far country to receive for himself a kingdom and then return. Calling ten of his servants, he gave them ten minas, and said to them, 'Engage in business until I come' " (Luke 19:12–13). There is no ownership in the kingdom, only stewardship. In fact, "How difficult it is for those who have wealth to enter the kingdom of God!" (Luke 18:24).

It is this land, this kingdom, that Jesus bestows on his messengers, the apostles, in Luke 22. Jesus knows the way of the world. "The kings of the Gentiles exercise lordship over them, and those in authority over them are called benefactors" (22:25). He understands the use and misuse of power and money. "But not so with you... You are those who have stayed with me in my trials, and I assign to you, as my Father assigned to me, a kingdom, that you may eat and drink at my table in my kingdom and sit on thrones judging the twelve tribes of Israel" (Luke 22:26–30). Jesus gave the Lord's Supper—the Passover meal fulfilled—as the central sign of this land-kingdom (Luke 22:14–23). Thus the land promise was fulfilled among his followers, in his kingdom. Now we turn to the extension of that kingdom by Jesus' apostles.

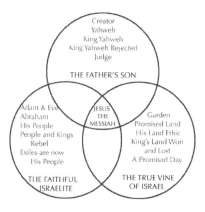

**Figure 9.** Fulfillment in Christ

## 7. Extension through Kingdom Outposts

Commissioned by Jesus and filled by his Spirit, the apostles launched the kingdom movement as recorded by Luke in Acts. In Acts 2, Peter announces the advent of "the last days" long predicted by the prophets—by the prophet Joel in particular (Joel 2:28–29). According to Peter, the coming of the Spirit to indwell "all flesh" is the sign of "the day of the Lord" (Acts 2:16–21). Cut to the heart by Peter's announcement, his audience pleaded for direction. Peter told them to repent, be baptized, and receive the Holy Spirit, "for the promise is for you and for your children and for all who are far off" (Acts 2:37–39). The sphere of blessing is no longer restricted to a land with geographical boundaries. The sphere of blessing has been extended beyond its fulfillment in Jesus of Nazareth. The sphere of blessing—the "place" of promise, the realm, the King's domain, the land—is now the new community of those who are baptized into Christ and receive his Spirit. Immediately 3,000 new followers of the Way begin "selling their possessions and belongings and distributing the proceeds to all, as any had need" (Acts 2:45). Further:

> There was not a needy person among them, for as many as were owners of lands or houses sold them and brought the proceeds of what was sold and laid it at the apostles' feet, and it was distributed to each as any had need. (Acts 4:34–35)

The echoes of the Torah—there shall be no poor among you in the land—are unmistakable. It was Jubilee in Jerusalem because the Spirit and Body of the Messiah were now there. A Kingdom Outpost had been planted in Jerusalem.

National Israel had been the locus of relief and development among the pagan nations. The Israelites' distinctive attitude toward land ownership, the poor, and the role of their kings and their wealth were meant to be a light, an example, to the Gentiles. Jesus fulfilled and embodied those values and taught a wilderness ethic of provision and money. In Acts, the locus of R&D living and ministry became the church that Jesus is building by his Spirit through his apostles (Matthew 16:18; Acts 1:8).

These apostles began to extend the movement. Sometimes they were forced outward by persecution. Sometimes they went out in response to the Holy Spirit's leading. Whether it was Peter among the Jews or Paul among the Gentiles, the message spread as they founded new communities of the Spirit. Acts records the spread of the gospel from Jerusalem to Rome, the center of the Roman Empire, from a poor woman named Mary and ordinary blue-collar fishermen to Caesar's household, from minority Jews to majority Gentiles. The spread of this movement took place through the formation of new communities—Kingdom Outposts—across the Roman Empire. The book of Acts is not simply the record of individual conversions; it is the record of the establishment of new little "societies of Jesus."

These Kingdom Outposts are designed to operate according to a different economy than the Egyptian, Canaanite, Babylonian, and now Roman economies we have surveyed already. Reflecting on Israel in Egypt and on the church today, Christopher Wright describes the intended economic life of these Kingdom Outposts:

> The sharpest pain of the oppression was economic. Israelites were being exploited as slave-labour, on land not their own, for the economic benefit of the host nation…
>
> …The objective of their redemption (also stated in Ex. 6:6–8) was to give them land of their own—along with an economic system that was intended to outlaw such oppression within Israel itself. As we will see in a moment, it was particularly in the economic realm that the Israelites themselves were to live redemptively, in response to what God had done for them…
>
> For that reason, we [the church] engage in redemptive living that seeks to bring the different dimensions of *God's* idea of redemption—as expressed in the Exodus and Year of Jubilee—

to bear on all such manifestations of oppression as surround us. And that is why we too must converse with Moses and the Elijah, for it is the Law and the Prophets that provide us with so many resources to put flesh and blood on what it means to live redemptively, to be moved by compassion, justice and generosity in a world of cruelty, exploitation and greed...

As we do so, we [the church] become communities that are like exodus and jubilee signposts, pointing to the redeeming work of God in the past and to the only hope of liberation that our world can have for the future. (Wright 2010, 100, 112–113)

In their written instructions to these young churches, the apostles were quite clear about the land or wilderness ethic of these Kingdom Outposts. In the Torah, the Israelites were not yet in the land, so the Lord taught them a wilderness ethic regarding food, caring for the poor, and economics. This ethic sustained them during their forty years in the wilderness. The wilderness ethic prepared them to occupy the land in which they were to live out the redemptive, economic land ethic that Wright describes in the above quote. The wilderness ethic is perhaps best symbolized by manna, which could not be hoarded but only eaten as daily bread. It's an ethic for a sojourning people who do not yet control their own land, but who are being prepared for that day. The land ethic is for a people who have arrived in the new land that God promised them; it is an extension or development of the wilderness ethic.

The church is a sojourning people (Colossians 3:1–4; James 4:4; 1 Peter 2:11). We live redemptively now in hope of the world that is to come—the new heaven and earth, which is our promised land (Revelation 21:22–27). We work and live now—distinctively from the surrounding world—in hope of the resurrection (1 Corinthians 15:58). Just as Yahweh prepared his sojourning people (Israel) through Moses and their years in the wilderness, so Jesus prepares his sojourning people (the church) through his Spirit and the teaching of his apostles as we live in anticipation of the whole creation's redemption (Romans 8:22–23).

What is this apostolic teaching? If you don't work, you don't eat. Laziness is not a kingdom virtue (2 Thessalonians 3:6–15). Families should be the first financial resource for widows and orphans, but the family of families—the Kingdom Outpost—should step in as needed (1 Timothy 5:3–8). Attention should be paid to the character of widows receiving financial help from the church; younger widows should get busy working and remarry and stay productive (1 Timothy 5:9–16). Economic relationships like that between master and slave are recast as family relationships (see Ephesians 6:5–9 and the letter of Philemon). Brothers who are slaves should show respect to brothers who are masters; masters should treat their slave-brothers as the Lord has treated them. At all times these new societies are to reject the idolatry of greed (Colossians 3:5). The way of the world is to be rejected (Ephesians 4:17). These Kingdom Outposts are not looking for a better financial future, defined along Roman and Greek lines. They are looking for a better city, a second advent, a new heaven and new earth, a heavenly Jerusalem to come to earth. In anticipation of this final consummation, these Kingdom Outposts will be communities of mercy and justice (Romans 12:8–13). They will be places of sharing and sufficiency (1 Corinthians 11:17–22). They will honor the poor (James 2:1–7). There will be no greedy rich among them (1 Timothy 6:17–19; James 5:1–6). All will be content in the Lord's presence (1 Timothy 6:3–10).

Their life together now is meant to be a sign of the soon-to-be consummated kingdom. These outposts are to "shine as lights" in a dark world (Philippians 2:15). Rather than practicing greed and the worship of wealth, they are to learn that "godliness with contentment is great gain" (1 Timothy 6:6) and that those who desire to get rich pierce themselves with grief and shipwreck their faith. Those who claim faith but ignore a brother in financial need are liars; the love of God is not in them (1 John 3:16–18). These communities of faith know that possessions and money are not the private capital of individual owners, but that a good steward uses work and money to advance the mission and bless these new societies of Jesus (Romans 16:1–3). Kingdom Outposts are to be sojourning communities marked by the hospitality of God (Romans 12:13, 20; 1 Timothy 3:2; Hebrews 13:2).

Further, these kingdom "demonstration projects" are tied to one another in the gospel (1 Thessalonians 1:2–10). Each local expression of the kingdom is networked together with other Kingdom Outposts across the empire through the ministry of apostolic teams (Philippians 1:3–14; 1 Timothy 1:3; Titus 1:5). Thus the apostle Paul can give the Corinthian outpost instructions for a church-based R&D project in Jerusalem:

> Now concerning the collection for the saints: as I directed the churches of Galatia, so you also are to do. On the first day of every week, each of you is to put something aside and store it up, as he may prosper, so that there will be no collecting when I come. And when I arrive, I will send those whom you accredit by letter to carry your gift to Jerusalem. If it seems advisable that I should go also, they will accompany me. (1 Corinthians 16:1–4)

In this particular case, the Jerusalem church was facing a famine. They needed relief. Paul gave the Corinthians yet further instructions:

> We want you to know, brothers, about the grace of God that has been given among the churches of Macedonia, for in a severe test of affliction, their abundance of joy and their extreme poverty have overflowed in a wealth of generosity on their part. For they gave according to their means, as I can testify, and beyond their means, of their own accord, begging us earnestly for the favor of taking part in the relief of the saints—and this, not as we expected, but they gave themselves first to the Lord and then by the will of God to us. Accordingly, we urged Titus that as he had started, so he should complete among you this act of grace. But as you excel in everything—in faith, in speech, in knowledge, in all earnestness, and in our love for you—see that you excel in this

act of grace also. I say this not as a command, but to prove by the earnestness of others that your love also is genuine. For you know the grace of our Lord Jesus Christ, that though he was rich, yet for your sake he became poor, so that you by his poverty might become rich. And in this matter I give my judgment: this benefits you, who a year ago started not only to do this work but also to desire to do it. So now finish doing it as well, so that your readiness in desiring it may be matched by your completing it out of what you have. For if the readiness is there, it is acceptable according to what a person has, not according to what he does not have. For I do not mean that others should be eased and you burdened, but that as a matter of fairness your abundance at the present time should supply their need, so that their abundance may supply your need, that there may be fairness. (2 Corinthians 8:1–14)

The "relief of the saints" is concerned with "fairness" or equality among God's people (2 Corinthians 8:13–14)—fairness in that no part of the body of Christ should suffer when another part of the body has plenty. Fairness so that those who have much should help those in need, and those in need can someday meet the needs of those presently in abundance. At the end of his exhortation, the apostle Paul reminds the Corinthians of the manna, the symbol of wilderness ethic: "Whoever gathered much had nothing left over, and whoever gathered little had no lack" (2 Corinthians 8:15; see also Exodus 16:18).

This is the apostolic vision of R&D in action. Within a local church there is sharing and fairness. Within networks of churches there is also sharing and fairness. Manna could not be hoarded in the wilderness or it spoiled. So too a Christian's—or a church's—money cannot be hoarded or it will spoil into greed, which is idolatry. Instead, we are called to use money to provide daily bread to meet the body of Christ's needs—trusting in God's provision for the future, not trusting in our ability to hoard.

The church's conduct as they attend to the "relief of the saints" not only supplies the needs of the family of God but also overflows into thanksgiving toward God. This generosity flows from "your confession of the gospel of Christ" (2 Corinthians 9:13). God has given us an "inexpressible gift" (9:15), so now we extend his gift to one another:

> The point is this: whoever sows sparingly will also reap sparingly, and whoever sows bountifully will also reap bountifully. Each one must give as he has decided in his heart, not reluctantly or under compulsion, for God loves a cheerful giver. And God is able to make all grace abound to you, so that having all sufficiency in all things at all times, you may abound in every good work. As it is written, "He has distributed freely, he has given to the poor; his righteousness endures forever." He who supplies seed to the sower and bread for food will supply and multiply your seed for sowing and increase the harvest of your righteousness. You will be enriched in every way to be generous in every way, which through us will

produce thanksgiving to God. For the ministry of this service is not only supplying the needs of the saints but is also overflowing in many thanksgivings to God. By their approval of this service, they will glorify God because of your submission that comes from your confession of the gospel of Christ, and the generosity of your contribution for them and for all others, while they long for you and pray for you, because of the surpassing grace of God upon you. Thanks be to God for his inexpressible gift! (2 Corinthians 9:6–15)

Jesus said that this good news of the inaugurated kingdom would be preached to all the peoples of the world, "and then the end will come" (Matthew 24:14). Luke's open-ended conclusion of Acts is clearly meant to teach us that we, led by the Spirit, are continuing to write that story, which in Luke's version ends with Paul "proclaiming the kingdom of God and teaching about the Lord Jesus Christ with all boldness and without hindrance" (Acts 28:31).

The three themes we traced through the promises of the Old Testament and their fulfillment in Christ are still alive in the New Testament. As the fulfillment of what was promised in the Old Testament, Jesus *was* Emmanuel, "God with us." He was the true, faithful Israelite who fulfilled the mission mandate, and was obedient even to death on a cross, exalted in his resurrection and ascension as the true King. The salvation that was once experienced by being "in the land" is now found by being "in Christ." And now, through the apostolic expansion of the kingdom—through establishing Kingdom Outposts—those blessings are being extended to the whole world.

God is now known as the Father of our Lord and Savior, Jesus the Messiah. Jesus Christ has himself been exalted above all others as Lord (Philippians 2:9–11). His people are now "one new man," a new race comprised of both Jews and Gentiles, forming a new temple with Messiah Jesus as "the cornerstone" (Ephesians 2:11–22). His people are, in fact, the body of Christ filled with the Spirit of Christ. As the community of faith has now extended into "every nation" as was promised to Abraham, so the land blessing has been extended. The Kingdom Outposts of Jesus are new heaven and new earth communities. They are designed to live now as the whole redeemed creation will live someday.

> An agrarian reading of the New Testament is possible and necessary... Any such reading of the New Testament will need to begin with an awareness of the agrarian perspective that dominates Israel's Scriptures, which are as indispensable for modern Christians as they were for the New Testament writers. Only a thorough understanding of how Israel represents the human place in the created order can enable Christians to delineate a responsible version of what partic-ipation in the renewal of creation might mean. (Davis 2009, 7)

The Kingdom Outposts will do this imperfectly, as the New Testament record shows. They can, however, live by a new economics well enough, so that they stand out like a city set on a hill. They can show that "life in the land" is possible, no matter where you are geographically, as long as you are together "in Christ" with his followers. To be "in Christ" is to be in his new community; it is to be part of a Kingdom Outpost of the coming promised land:

> "And yet I confess that I have come to feel that the primary reality of which we have to take account in seeking for a Christian impact on public life is the Christian congregation. How is it possible that the gospel should be credible, that people should come to believe that the power which has the last word in human affairs is represented by a man hanging on a cross? I am suggesting that the only answer, the only hermeneutic of the gospel, is a congregation of men and women who believe it and live by it... Jesus, as I said earlier, did not write a book but formed a community." (Newbigin 1989, 227)

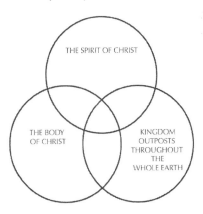

**Figure 10.** Extension through Kingdom Outposts

## 8. Final Consummation

All creation, which at present groans for the "revealing of the sons of God" (Romans 8:19), will be redeemed. Jubilee will be consummated, but not just in geographical Israel. The whole earth will be covered with the glory of God:

> He has delivered us from the domain of darkness and transferred us to the kingdom of his beloved Son, in whom we have redemption, the forgiveness of sins. He is the image of the invisible God, the firstborn of all creation. For by him all things were created, in heaven and on earth, visible and invisible, whether thrones or dominions or rulers or authorities—all things were created through him and for him. And he is before all things, and in him all things hold together. And he is the head of the body, the church. He is the beginning, the firstborn from the dead, that in everything he might be preeminent. For in him all the fullness of God was pleased to dwell, and through him to reconcile to himself all things, whether on earth or in heaven, making peace by the blood of his cross. And you, who once were alienated and hostile in mind, doing evil deeds, he has now reconciled in his body of flesh by his death, in order to present you holy and blameless and above reproach before him, if indeed you continue in the faith, stable and steadfast, not shifting from the hope of the gospel that you heard, which has been proclaimed in all creation

under heaven, and of which I, Paul, became a minister. (Colossians 1:13–23)

While right now we are "sojourners and exiles" (1 Peter 2:11) living by a wilderness ethic—pilgrims on a journey, heirs who have only received so far the "guarantee of our inheritance until we acquire possession of it" (Ephesians 1:14)—we look forward to the extension of the land promise "in Christ" fulfilled in the whole earth:

> Grace to you and peace from God our Father and the Lord Jesus Christ. Blessed be the God and Father of our Lord Jesus Christ, who has blessed us *in Christ* with every spiritual blessing in the heavenly places, even as he chose us *in him* before the foundation of the world, that we should be holy and blameless *before him*. In love he predestined us for adoption as sons *through Jesus Christ*, according to the purpose of his will, to the praise of his glorious grace, with which he has blessed *us in the Beloved*. *In him* we have redemption through his blood, the forgiveness of our trespasses, according to the riches of his grace, which he lavished upon us, in all wisdom and insight making known to us the mystery of his will, according to his purpose, which he set forth *in Christ* as a plan for the fullness of time, to unite all things *in him*, things in heaven and things on earth. *In him* we have obtained an inheritance, having been predestined according to the purpose of him who works all things according to the counsel of his will, so that we

who were the first to hope *in Christ* might be to the praise of his glory. *In him* you also, when you heard the word of truth, the gospel of your salvation, and believed *in him*, were sealed with the promised Holy Spirit, who is the guarantee of our inheritance until we acquire possession of it, to the praise of his glory. (Ephesians 1:2–14, emphasis added)

We live in anticipation of the new earth, which will come down from heaven:

Then I saw a new heaven and a new earth, for the first heaven and the first earth had passed away, and the sea was no more. And I saw the holy city, new Jerusalem, coming down out of heaven from God, prepared as a bride adorned for her husband. And I heard a loud voice from the throne saying, "Behold, the dwelling place of God is with man. He will dwell with them, and they will be his people, and God himself will be with them as their God. He will wipe away every tear from their eyes, and death shall be no more, neither shall there be mourning, nor crying, nor pain anymore, for the former things have passed away." (Revelation 21:1–4)

Then the angel showed me the river of the water of life, bright as crystal, flowing from the throne of God and of the Lamb through the middle of the street of the city; also, on either side of the river, the tree of life with its twelve kinds of fruit, yielding its fruit each month. The leaves of the tree were for the healing of the nations.

No longer will there be anything accursed, but the throne of God and of the Lamb will be in it, and his servants will worship him. They will see his face, and his name will be on their foreheads. And night will be no more. They will need no light of lamp or sun, for the Lord God will be their light, and they will reign forever and ever. (Revelation 22:1–5)

And so our storied, biblical theology of relief and development is complete.

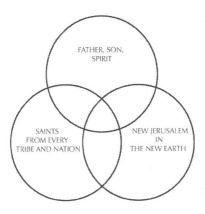

**Figure 11.** Final Consummation

## Summary

Put simply, the biblical concept of relief and development is that new communities of God's people are planted across the globe. In every tribe and civilization, these Kingdom Outposts live out a new economics, a fair and just approach to sharing, a stewardship of the earth and its gifts. They live out the way of Christ and his apostles. They are more than a source of money and people. They are more than demonstration projects. They are the actual locus, the actual location, of R&D.

Said differently, to come into the life of that new Kingdom Outpost is to enter into a salvation that begins now in the before-afterlife, continues into the afterlife, and is consummated in the after-afterlife resurrection and the new earth at the end of history. Eternal R&D.

This means that what we often call "church planting" is the primary biblical strategy for doing R&D. *But not just any "church" will do.* It must be a local church, connected to other churches through an apostolic network, and grounded in the apostolic teaching about money, economics, and poverty as outlined in this chapter. It must be a Kingdom Outpost.

Unlike some conventional R&D projects by Christians, kingdom economics cannot be separated from the daily life of Christians together. I have been on numerous short-term mission trips, and my experience has been that many participants are surprised by the intensity of their spiritual experiences while on these trips, as compared to their experiences at home. I'm sure there are many reasons for this. I'm also sure that one of those reasons is that they've had a taste of kingdom economics and living on these trips. They've sacrificed time and money. They've devoted themselves to helping the poor for a week. They've shared of themselves and their wealth. But then they came home and too often began living once more by the rules of a capitalist economy, which does not believe the love of money is the root of all evil. They've come back to a society where even in the church it's every person for himself, economically speaking. They've returned to an economy that says those of us with means are all deserving owners, and the poor are just lazy. They've reentered an economy that believes that we earned our wealth, and that our wealth is most certainly not a gift from God to be stewarded for the benefit of others. If we are religious, we might give some of our wealth to charity or the church. But it's ours, as far as we're concerned.

In contrast, each of the eight promises described in this chapter offers a wealth of teaching about God's economics. Here's one way to summarize this teaching, in light of the topic of R&D. Each point corresponds to one of the eight promises of our framework in order:

1. God's vision is an agrarian vision, not an industrialist vision, as we saw in chapter one. Creation is not a machine or a mine to be exploited for profit. Creation is a sacred garden, meant to be received as a gift and tended and stewarded respectfully.

2. Though humanity rejects this vision, God reaffirms his intent to bless everyone on earth. God intends to relieve our misery and redevelop our world, so that we are all blessed. God is on an R&D mission.

3. God's obedient people forsake economies based on ownership and oppression (whether communist, socialist, or capitalist) and embrace an economy of stewardship characterized by sharing, not hoarding. God's people welcome anyone into their new economy. They are the locus of blessing and shalom of R&D living.

4. Those of God's people to whom he has entrusted power, wealth, and opportunity are called to use these blessings to spread justice and righteousness among all people within their God-given sphere of influence. Economic leaders don't lord it over others; they serve others.

5. Economics and our use of wealth are inextricably connected to true worship, fidelity to God's Word, and enjoyment of his blessing. There is no sacred and secular divide. R&D is a spiritual issue. Injustice, the selfish use of wealth, and mistreatment of the poor among God's people will all be cause for discipline from our Father.

6. Jesus Christ embodied, fulfilled, and taught his Father's economics, fully intending that his disciples would not only look to him for an afterlife salvation but also follow him and his before-afterlife teaching—that they would worship God, not wealth, in their politics and economics:

> It cannot mean that the Church is seen as a voluntary society of individuals who have decided to follow Jesus in their personal lives, a society which does not challenge the assumptions which govern the worlds of politics, economics, education, and culture. The model for all Christian discipleship is given once and for all in the ministry of Jesus. His ministry entailed the calling of

individual men and women to personal and costly discipleship, but at the same time it challenged the principalities and powers, the ruler of this world, and the cross was the price paid for that challenge. Christian discipleship today cannot mean less than that. (Newbigin 1989, 220)

7. Jesus' people, now including people from every nation, are meant to once again live out his economics as a light to the world. Christ's apostles taught the churches a compelling vision for a distinctive economic way of life together. These economic principles include cash transfers from church to church through apostolic networks and trusted leaders. This way of life spreads across the world not through conventional R&D projects but through the establishment of new, distinctive communities—Kingdom Outposts. This is the way of Christ and his apostles for R&D.

8. Although kingdom economics is a minority view in the world, we are called to live it faithfully and in the sure and certain hope of the resurrection, at which time it will become the economics of the new earth.

The biblical theology traced in this chapter leads to the following evaluative criteria for any approach to R&D or theology of R&D:

1. Are local churches conceived of as the very locus of R&D? Or are they merely understood as sources of money and manpower?

2. Are local churches conceived of as Kingdom Outposts—in other words, is their life together characterized by kingdom values, economics, and relationships? Is R&D accomplished by multiplying these outposts?

3. Are local churches understood to be part of broader apostolic networks? Are these church-to-church relationships characterized by kingdom fairness and the sharing of resources with one another?

4. Is R&D understood as part of salvation, a salvation that is carried to nations and civilizations by the planting and establishing of new Kingdom Outposts?

5. Is the underlying economic mind-set one of kingdom stewardship or pagan ownership? Is the attitude toward the earth, its creatures, and its gifts one of western desacralized industrialism, or is it one of agrarian care for the sacred in the image of the land's owner?

The next chapter will apply these evaluative questions to current R&D literature and concepts.

# CHAPTER THREE

# A SURVEY AND EVALUATION OF CURRENT RELIEF AND DEVELOPMENT LITERATURE

There has been a flood of literature about R&D the last fifteen years. The topic is so popular, and the conversation so current, that the dialogue is being carried forward in a plethora of monographs and essay collections. The academic conversation—and in particular the evangelical academic conversation (as noted in chapter one)—seems to be lagging behind the marketplace conversation. This chapter is both a survey and an evaluation of the current conversation, using the summary questions and perspective from the end of the previous chapter.

Two categories of recent literature will be surveyed and evaluated in light of the storied theology and themes of chapter two. We will review recent evangelical works and recent marketplace works that address either R&D in general or aid to Haiti in particular. Over the last ten years or so, we have witnessed a flourishing of literature that critiques existing aid and R&D efforts. Some of this literature takes on the nature of an exposé. Other works present alternative models or suggested improvements. There is a growing consensus, both in evangelicalism and in the marketplace, that the current system of aid is at best inefficient and somewhat ineffective, and at worst corrupt and destructive.

## Recent Evangelical Literature

The following ten works cover these subjects: current practices, imperialistic or dependency-producing approaches, informing theology, microfinance solutions, business-as-mission (BAM), true partnership approaches to R&D, and participation strategies that run from local to global. These works represent the best thinking in evangelicalism right now.

1. *When Helping Hurts: How to Alleviate Poverty Without Hurting the Poor... and Yourself* by Steve Corbett and Brian Fikkert (2009). Both men are professors of economics at Covenant College. Dr. Fikkert is the founder and executive director of the Chalmers Center for Economic Development. Theirs is a seminal book that has become widely used in evangelical churches. With a rigorous Reformed theological underpinning, the book presents in popular terms a much deeper biblical understanding of poverty, and it points toward alternatives to some of the current approaches to R&D.

2. *Fast Living: How the Church Will End Extreme Poverty* by Scott Todd, PhD (2011), senior ministry advisor for Compassion International. This book is something of a manifesto

for Compassion International, and it is self-consciously "church-based." It is intended to be a call to action for American evangelicals to "fast" with their lives and resources and give the surplus to the poor, hence the title. It represents a large parachurch organization's effort to take seriously the role of the American local church in global poverty reduction.

3. *God of the Empty-Handed: Poverty, Power and the Kingdom of God* by Jayakumar Christian, PhD (1999), associate director of World Vision India, North Zone. Christian has his doctorate in intercultural studies from Fuller Theological Seminary. As an Indian theologian, he approaches the subject from a developing world perspective. The book is a survey of the R&D landscape and its assumptions, followed by an extended presentation of the most biblical kingdom perspective I've encountered in my research. It is noteworthy that this fine work was done by someone outside North American evangelicalism.

4. *God Is At Work: Transforming People and Nations Through Business* by Ken Eldred (2009), CEO of Living Stones Foundation. Eldred's book was named the number one book on kingdom business by the Business as Mission Network in 2005 and 2009. It presents a mixture of decent theological reflection and shallow pragmatism. Nevertheless, it is considered one of the flagship books of the BAM movement, and it is a useful introduction to the ideas (and lack of depth) prevalent in this arena.

5. *The Hole in Our Gospel: What Does God Expect of Us?The Answer That Changed My Life and Might Just Change the World* by Richard Stearns (2010), president of World Vision USA. This book was named the 2010 Christian Book of the Year. It is a manifesto for World Vision and a wake-up call intended for a wealthy, complacent North American church. That this comes from a respected former CEO of a major corporation, who is now the CEO of the world's largest evangelical NGO, adds to its weight. Though written at a popular level, Stearns's book is well researched and is theologically competent.

6. *My Business, My Mission: Fighting Poverty Through Partnerships* by Doug Seebeck and Timothy Stoner (2009). Seebeck is the founder and president of Partners Worldwide. This fine book is not intended as a theological treatise; rather it makes the case for job creation and marketplace partnerships across cultures as a viable kingdom enterprise—one that brings blessing to the poor and to their wealthy partners.

7. *The Poor Will Be Glad: Joining the Revolution to Lift the World Out of Poverty* by Peter Greer and Phil Smith (2009). Greer is president of HOPE International, a global faith-based microfinance organization. Smith is a private investor and philanthropist. Their collaborative book provides a very good survey of the need, current landscape, and emerging R&D strategies within evangelical Christianity. It does an

excellent job of including local churches in its strategies, and it is refreshingly honest about the challenges of parachurch-church partnerships.

8. *Toxic Charity: How Churches and Charities Hurt Those They Help (And How to Reverse It)* by Robert D. Lupton (2011). Lupton is the founder and president of Focused Community Strategies Urban Ministries. This book is primarily written from an American inner-city perspective. Lupton does an excellent job documenting the unintended consequences of so many poverty alleviation efforts in the United States. The lessons apply internationally as well.

9. *Walking with the Poor: Principles and Practices of Transformational Development* by Bryant L. Meyers (2011), professor of transformational development at Fuller Theological Seminary and past vice president for international program strategy at World Vision International. This book is deep and broad and in the same league as Jayakumar Christian's *God of the Empty-Handed*. It is written by a North American who has rich international experience and a deep grounding in both theology and R&D.

10. *When Charity Destroys Dignity: Overcoming Unhealthy Dependency in the Christian Movement* by Glenn Schwartz (2007), executive director of World Mission Associates and past administrator in the School of World Mission at Fuller Theological Seminary. Schwartz's book, a highly detailed analysis of typical missionary efforts and charities and their unintended

consequences, is very helpful in exploring the relational aspects of missions and the dangers of colonialism and dependency.

The oldest of these ten monographs was released in 1999. The other nine have been published within the last five years.

## Marketplace Literature

As in evangelical publishing, there has been an explosion of literature about R&D in the broader marketplace. There is a vigorous debate on how to proceed with R&D, yet there seems to be broad agreement on the failures of past responses to poverty. Eleven recent monographs and essay collections represent the current conversation well.

1. *Pyramids of Sacrifice: Political Ethics and Social Change* by Peter Berger (1976). Berger's insights into the quasi-religious function of social engineering and R&D efforts are priceless, even though it is the oldest work surveyed in this chapter.

2. *Just Give Money to the Poor: The Development Revolution from the Global South* by Joseph Hanlon, Armando Barrientos, and David Hulme (2010). The authors provide a remarkably fresh perspective that posits cash transfers—directly giving cash to poor people—as the best possible solution to global poverty. They debunk Western assumptions about the poor and the perceived dangers of just giving them money.

3. *Culture Matters: How Values Shape Human Progress*, edited by Lawrence Harrison and Samuel Huntington (2000). This is a collection of essays on the impact of values and culture on poverty and development. The essays constitute something of a manifesto in the R&D world, where for several decades it was politically incorrect to consider culture as a contributor to poverty. Past abuses of racial stereotyping and cultural arrogance notwithstanding, the contributors make a convincing case that changing a culture can be a major factor in alleviating poverty.

4. *Helping People Help Themselves: From the World Bank to an Alternative Philosophy* of Development Assistance by David Ellerman (2005). Ellerman, an economic advisor to the World Bank and a visiting scholar at the University of California at Riverside, provides a critique of aid. His rigorous theory and humanistic outlook combine to make the case that while the wrong kind of help creates unintended dependency, indirect aid can truly empower people and societies to help themselves.

5. *Dead Aid: Why Aid Is Not Working and How There Is a Better Way for Africa* by Dambisa Moyo (2009). This book is a blistering critique of aid to Africa, written by an African woman who is an economist, a Goldman Sachs employee, and a World Bank advisor. Moyo is unrelenting in her opposition to more aid for Africa and calls for an African-led development program instead.

6. *Travesty in Haiti: A True Account of Christian Missions, Orphanages, Fraud, Food Aid and Drug Trafficking* by Timothy Schwartz (2010). Schwartz's book is a compilation of his own firsthand observations and secondhand anecdotes about the results of R&D in Haiti. The book, an exposé of aid fraud in Haiti, is not so much a reasoned argument as it is a series of negative illustrations of the alleged problems with NGOs in Haiti.

7. *The Bottom Billion: Why the Poorest Countries are Failing and What Can Be Done About It* by Paul Collier (2007). Collier provides analysis of "poverty traps" that keep some countries mired in destitution. Arguably one of the "big three" of the marketplace authors, Collier contends that we have a huge emerging problem concerning the one billion people who seem to be permanently stuck in poverty. His idea of "poverty traps" has been critiqued as undermining personal and cultural responsibility, but the main idea has become a framework adopted by many other thinkers.

8. *The End of Poverty: Economic Possibilities for Our Time* by Jeffrey Sachs (2005). This book presented a proposal to end extreme poverty through more, not less, aid. The second of the "big three" marketplace authors, Sachs is unabashedly a proponent of one more "big push" to end poverty. This big push will need lots of money from Western governments and will be administered primarily through a multitude

of United Nations agencies. Call it an all-out, top-down, from-the-West-to-the-rest solution.

9. *The White Man's Burden: Why the West's Efforts to Aid the Rest Have Done So Much Ill and So Little Good* by William Easterly (2006). This is the "conservative" response to Sachs, contending that one more big push is not the answer, capitalism is. As the third of the "big three" marketplace authors, Easterly calls for a more scientific, case-study-based approach that would result in many smaller local projects to alleviate poverty.

10. *Poor Economics: Radical Rethinking of the Way to Fight Global Poverty* by Abhijit Banerjee and Esther Duflo (2011). *Poor Economics* is a critique of both Sachs and Easterly from a developing world perspective. Important for its non-Western vantage point, the book essentially rejects any "big answers," whether they come from progressives or conservatives. Instead, Banerjee and Duflo call for scientific, carefully run, local experiments in R&D, implementing ideas generated by local communities and leaders.

11. *The Road to Hell: The Ravaging Effects of Foreign Aid and International Charity* by Michael Maren (1997). This is another negative critique of how international aid works and how—in Maren's opinion—it corrupts. Maren offers a personal account of his experiences in Africa working first for the Peace Corps, then Catholic Relief Services, and finally USAID.

Note again how recent most of these works are. Apart from Berger's book, each has been published in the last fifteen years, with several having been published very recently.

## Organization of the Survey

As I researched the aforementioned literature with the biblical theology of chapter two in mind, it seemed to organize itself into four major categories, addressing issues from different perspectives. Each category included both evangelical and marketplace authors, all of whom had a wide variety of suggestions and solutions to offer. Of the many issues addressed in the literature, these four seemed most germane to my thesis:

1. *Critique of past and current R&D efforts.* Because there is a growing consensus on many of the failures of past approaches, the literature can inform an effective biblical approach to R&D, perhaps minimizing unintended consequences.

2. *Two paths: from the top down or from the bottom up?* An ongoing debate in the marketplace literature is whether we need even bigger, top-down solutions or small, local, bottom-up solutions. Some of the evangelical literature assumes a top-down (or "the West knows best") approach, an approach heavily critiqued in much of the secular literature. Establishing Kingdom Outposts is a bottom-up endeavor, as these are local, apostolically established communities living out a kingdom economics as salt and light in a local culture.

3. *Guilty secret: the role of values, religion, and culture.* This concern, which was overlooked for a long time, has made a comeback. It is particularly important for a Kingdom Outpost perspective, as Kingdom Outposts are all about values, religion, and culture formation.

4. *The invisible church.* The church is not quite invisible in the literature surveyed. It's barely visible, scattered here and there. It might be more accurate to say that remarks about the church range from dismay on the part of secular authors that the church might have some role to play, to evangelical authors who almost without exception ignore the local church as a major player in R&D. The church's role in these conversations is weak and nearly invisible.

The survey of the literature will be organized around these four issues. At the end of this chapter, I will offer an overall summary using the five questions from the end of chapter two.

# 1. Critique of Past and Current R&D Efforts

A major portion of the recent flourishing of R&D literature has criticized the "development industry" and the overall system of international aid. Just a survey of the titles gives the flavor of this critique: *Dead Aid, Toxic Charity, When Helping Hurts, When Charity Destroys Dignity, Travesty in Haiti,* and *The Road to Hell.* There is a growing view in both evangelical and marketplace literature that current aid and development efforts are misguided at best, and at worst may actually cause human suffering.

The statistics are staggering and admittedly a bit mind-numbing. In her book *Dead Aid*, Dambisa Moyo focuses largely on government-to-government loans and grants, not emergency or charity-based aid (though she's not a fan of either). Her accounting of government aid to the continent of Africa is representative of the kind of statistics quoted in this literature:

> So there we have it: sixty years, over US$1 trillion dollars of African aid, and not much good to show for it. Were aid simply innocuous—just not doing what it claimed it would do—this book would not have been written. The problem is that aid is not benign—it's malignant. No longer part of the potential solution, it's part of the problem— in fact aid is the problem. (Moyo 2009, 47)

Her book then goes on to document in compelling terms how aid fosters systemic corruption, erodes social trust-capital, encourages civil war, competes with domestic production, chokes off exports, and creates a culture of dependency.

At the other end of the spectrum from large government-to-government aid are the thousands of small NGOs active in countries like Haiti. These NGOs are drilling wells, starting schools, sponsoring children, building homes and church buildings, and carrying out countless other well-intentioned projects. Schwartz's book *Travesty in Haiti* is a non-stop exposé of the fraud, corruption, and even drug trafficking endemic in the "republic of NGOs" that is Haiti. One entire chapter is dedicated to "Orphans With Parents and Other Scams that Bilk U.S. Churchgoers." Throughout Haiti the typical small-NGO model is a church-school-orphanage. As one longtime Haitian resident told me, however, the first thing you have to realize is that "churches, schools, and orphanages are family businesses in Haiti, not nonprofit charities." Schwartz claims that many of these "orphanages" actually house children with living Haitian parents, children who are sponsored by well-meaning Christians in the United States.

While there are shining examples of well-intentioned and well-delivered NGO efforts in Haiti, it is impossible to dispute Schwartz's summary statement from *Travesty*:

> But while individual NGOs have educated children, drilled wells, planted trees, and saved tens of thousands of lives through vaccination and clinic programs; they have accomplished little detectable change in the country as a whole. Haiti remains the most underdeveloped nation in the Western hemisphere and over the past three decades, *precisely when NGO activity flourished*, it has sunk further into abysmal poverty. (Schwartz 2010, Appendix H, emphasis added)

While the lack of progress in Haiti, with its over 9,000 NGOs, does not demonstrate that aid never works, it does call into question how R&D is being done there. Quotations of this genre could go on and on.

Perhaps two more quotes highlight one of the main problems with aid—it is too often rooted in a colonial mind-set:

In Africa, the people who are supposed to benefit from aid see what is happening. They hear foreigners talking about development, but they know development was a colonial policy. Development was a policy of subjugation. When colonials came ashore, they didn't say, "We're here to steal your land and take your resources and employ your people to clean our toilets and guard our big houses." They said, "We're here to help you." And then they went and took their land and resources and hired people to clean their toilets. And now here come the aid workers, who move into the big colonial houses and ride in high cars above the squalor, all the while insisting they've come to help. (Maren 1997, 11)

Dr. Brian Fikkert addresses the same issue from a biblical viewpoint, talking about the god complex of many well-intentioned helpers:

One of the major premises of this book is *that until we embrace our mutual brokenness, our work with low-income people is likely to do far more harm than good...* the economically rich often have "god-complexes," a subtle and unconscious sense of superiority in which they believe that they have achieved their wealth through their own efforts and that they have been anointed to decide what is best for low-income people, whom they view as inferior to themselves...

And now we have come to a very central point: *one of the biggest problems in many poverty-alleviation efforts is that their design and implementation exacerbates the poverty of being of the economically rich—their god-complexes—and the poverty of being of the economically poor—their feelings of inferiority and shame.* (Corbett and Fikkert 2009, 64–65)

R&D can be—but need not be—destructive to both the helper and the helped. This is also the point of Ellerman's *Helping People Help Themselves*. One should not reach the conclusion that we should never help the poor, provide relief to the suffering, or assist in economic development. After all, these are the goals of the HaitiCure project detailed in the next chapter. However, we must be smarter in how we go about doing R&D work. R&D is complex. The issues are manifold. Simplistic solutions often make things worse. The unintended consequences of well-intentioned efforts can be devastating.

A second underlying problem with aid, attested to in both the evangelical and marketplace literature, is a failure to distinguish between necessary short-term relief and the slower, more difficult, longer-term work of development. Note this quote from the marketplace:

The second form of unhelpful help occurs when the helper undercuts self-help by inadvertently supplying the motivation for the doer to be in or remain in a condition to receive help. One prominent form is long-term charitable relief. The world is awash with disaster situations that call for various forms of short-term charitable relief. The point is not to oppose short-term relief operations but to understand how charitable relief operates in the longer term to erode the doers' incentives to help themselves—and thus it creates a dependency relationship. Charity corrupts; long-term charity corrupts long-term. Such help creates a generalized form of "moral hazard"— *instead of enabling self-help, it becomes a perverse dependency-creating alternative to self-help.* Charitable relief in the longer term is an "undercutting" form of unhelpful help. (Ellerman 2005, 12–13, emphasis added).

And this from an evangelical perspective:

One of the biggest mistakes that North American churches make—by far—is in applying relief in situations in which rehabilitation or development is the appropriate intervention. (Corbett and Fikkert 2009, 105).

Fikkert identifies three stages of poverty alleviation efforts: relief, rehabilitation, and development. Relief consists of urgent and temporary emergency aid. Rehabilitation begins "as soon as the bleeding stops" and is an interim step to help a community get back on its feet. Development is the long-term process of creating a sustainable, prosperous economy. It is something "not done *to* people or *for* people but *with* people. *The key dynamic in development is promoting an empowering process* in which all the people involved… become more of what God created them to be" (104–105, emphasis added).

The authors of *Toxic Charity* have observed the following:

Our compassionate instinct has a serious shortcoming. Our memory is short when recovery is long. We respond with immediacy to desperate circumstances but often are unable to shift from crisis relief to the more complex work of long-term development. Consequently, aid agencies tend to prolong the "emergency" status of a crisis when a rebuilding strategy should be well under way...

...When relief does not transition to development in a timely way, compassion becomes toxic...

Doing *for* rather than doing *with* those in need is the norm. Add to it the combination of patronizing pity and unintended superiority, and charity becomes toxic...

...Yes, there are Haiti earthquakes. But the overwhelming majority of our mission trips are to places where the needs are for development rather than emergency assistance. And development is about enabling indigenous people to help themselves. (Lupton, 6–7, 35, 69)

There is a growing consensus in the literature that (1) aid conceived of as never-ending handouts does not work but actually harms the people it seeks to help; (2) donor attitudes are as much a part of the problem as recipient attitudes, with the former often falling prey to colonial or god-complex attitudes; and (3) aid that does not distinguish adequately between short-term relief and long-term development must be radically altered, or should cease outright.

This raises the question: how should development be done? Perhaps the growing discontent with past approaches to development represents a window of opportunity to demonstrate a better way. Our world and our poor are ready for something better, something that actually works, something that actually brings peace and salvation from poverty.

## 2. Two Paths: From the Top Down or from the Bottom Up?

A debate is raging in the secular literature over this question. Do we need even more and even larger aid projects in order to get over the hump and eradicate poverty, or do we need to end large, top-down schemes and focus on local, smaller, bottom-up initiatives? This argument is primarily a northern hemisphere argument, concentrated in the United States and Europe. More recently, southern hemisphere economists and theologians have been weighing in with a very different perspective. Within evangelical literature, the discussion is around similar but not identical issues—namely, the use and abuse of North American short-term missions as a development strategy, the role of businesses and job creation efforts, the effectiveness of child sponsorship initiatives, and partnership strategies that empower indigenous people and churches.

Currently, the leading spokesmen in the northern secular debate are Paul Collier, author of *The Bottom Billion*; Jeffrey Sachs, author of *The End of Poverty*; and William Easterly, author of *The White Man's Burden*.

They each have impeccable credentials, and each takes a distinct position.

Sachs is the proponent of even more aid, delivered from rich countries in "one big push" that could eradicate poverty in our time. He believes the poorest nations are locked in "poverty traps" they cannot escape from without significant outside help. He was special advisor to the United Nations on the Millennium Development Goals, which are meant to be achieved by 2015. Sachs wants rich countries to increase their aid to 0.7 percent of their gross domestic product (in the United States it is currently at about 0.18 percent). This increased funding would be administered through an improved network of large existing aid institutions such as the World Bank, the International Monetary Fund, and several United Nations agencies. Sachs unapologetically advocates for central planning—a top-down approach he calls "Enlightened Globalization":

> [It is] a globalization that addresses the needs of the poorest of the poor, the global environment, and the spread of democracy. It is the kind of global-ization championed by the Enlightenment—a globalization of democracies, multilateralism, science and technology, and a global economic system designed to meet human needs. We could call this an Enlightened Globalization. (Sachs 2005, 358)

Sachs's foremost critic is William Easterly. Easterly devotes an entire chapter of *White Man's Burden* to refuting Sachs's thesis. In this chapter, titled "The Legend of the Big Push," Easterly writes the following:

Unfortunately, the stubborn survival of the legend of the Big Push, despite evidence of its failure, has continued to foster the planning approach to development. The Planners' response to failure of previous interventions was to do even more intensive and comprehensive interventions. (Easterly 2006, 55)

Easterly believes the "big push" approach is rooted in a colonial mind-set—"the West knows best for the rest!"—or what he calls "utopian social planning." He proposes replacing this approach with a searcher mind-set. Searchers are innovators who live close to the problems of poverty and try—over and over again if necessary—smaller, localized solutions to end poverty. Easterly rejects the assumption that there is one overarching utopian theory or solution. He also is a fan of the Enlightenment (that is, modernity), but more so of its experimental scientific method than its philosophical underpinnings:

The sad part is the poor have had so little power to hold agencies accountable that the aid agencies have not had enough incentive to find out what works and what the poor actually want. The most important suggestion is to *search* for small improvements, then brutally scrutinize and test whether the poor got what they wanted and were better off, and then repeat the process. (Easterly 2006, 206)

Easterly's bottom-up approach rejects the idea of a "poverty trap" (38–44). He recognizes that there are indeed obstacles and entrenched problems to be

➤ Any / All wk
w/ Churches
Concrete detail
like w expanding
Using Verbs?
Advance Conversation?

---

Review MLK Place
ministry 4 steps to
Bless

overcome, but he notes the rise of many nations to developed status by efforts from within, not by a big push from outside. Easterly's approach emphasizes the role of the individual:

> The utopian agenda has led to collective responsibility for multiple goals for each agency, one of the worst incentive systems invented since mankind started walking upright...
>
> ...The aim should be to make individuals better off, not to transform governments or societies...
>
> Remember, aid cannot achieve the end of poverty. Only homegrown development based on the dynamism of individuals and firms in free markets can do that...
>
> Put the focus back where it belongs: get the poorest people in the world such obvious goods as the vaccines, the antibiotics, the food supplements, the improved seeds, the fertilizer, the roads, the boreholes, the water pipes, the textbooks, and the nurses. This is not making the poor dependent on handouts; it is giving the poorest people the health, nutrition, education and other inputs that raise the payoff to their own efforts to better their lives...
>
> ...Have individual accountability for individual tasks. (Easterly 2006, 368–369)

Easterly says, "The only Big Answer is that there is no Big Answer." Only a bottom-up solution will eradicate poverty:

Aid won't make poverty history, which Western aid efforts cannot possibly do. Only the self-reliant efforts of poor people and poor societies themselves can end poverty, borrowing ideas and institutions from the West when it suits them to do so. But aid that concentrates on feasible tasks will alleviate the sufferings of many desperate people in the meantime. Isn't that enough? (Easterly 2006, 383)

The third major voice in the northern debate is Paul Collier, author of *The Bottom Billion*. Collier's main contribution is in focusing on the one billion people who are stuck, "living and dying in fourteenth-century conditions." We used to think of one billion wealthy people in the world who should be concerned about the five billion poor people. Collier documents that 80 percent of those five billion people live in countries and places that are, in fact, currently developing and improving.

However, there are one billion people who are stuck in "poverty traps," to borrow Sachs's phrase (Collier 2007, 5–11). These people are trapped in countries with bad governance, bad geography, chronic war or conflict, and natural resources that have enriched the elites while impoverishing everyone else. These one billion people are being left behind, and in some cases their situation is worsening. Most of the fifty-eight countries where these poverty traps exist are in Africa and Central Asia:

Seventy percent of these people are in Africa, and most Africans are living in countries that have been in one or another of the traps. Africa is therefore the core of the problem... [However,] the countries of the bottom billion do not form a group with a convenient geographic label. When I want to use a geographic label for them I describe them as "Africa +," with the + being places such as *Haiti*, Bolivia, the Central Asian countries, Laos, Cambodia, Yemen, Burma and North Korea. (Collier 2007, 7, emphasis added).

While Collier is a top-down proponent, he proposes large solutions of a different sort than Sachs. Rather than large government aid projects, Collier proposes better trade policies, security strategies, and changes in law and in international charters. He goes so far as to propose military intervention by the wealthy countries, working multilaterally, to stabilize some of the bottom fifty-eight countries. In this respect, he is very much a "West knows best for the rest" kind of economist. On the other hand, he says something that sounds very like Easterly:

Unfortunately, it is not just about giving these countries our money. If it were, it would be relatively easy because there are not many of them. With some important exceptions, aid does not work so well in these environments, at least as it has been provided in the past. Change in the societies at the very bottom must come predominantly from within; we cannot impose it on them. (Collier 2007, xi)

Collier's point is that the argument between the top-down and bottom-up camps does not apply to the bottom billion. Their situation is so uniquely desperate that completely different measures—including, in some cases, military intervention—are necessary. His proposed measures focus on creating safe environments in which local heroes can solve their own problems. According to Collier, we are using aid badly: "The aid agencies are not run by fools; they are full of intelligent people severely constrained by what public opinion permits" (Collier 2007, 184). Like Sachs, Collier believes we will continue to need aid on a large scale, just used more wisely. He argues we are not using the instruments of security, laws, and charters at all to help these one billion people at the bottom.

Collier believes Sachs "has overplayed the importance of aid" and ignored these wider policy suggestions. And he believes that Easterly "exaggerates the downside [of aid] and again neglects the scope for other policies." In summary, "we need to narrow the target [to the bottom billion] and broaden the instruments" (Collier 2007, 191–192).

There are two recent authors from the Global South who have joined the conversation. The first is a blended perspective from Banerjee and Duflo called *Poor Economics*. Banerjee was educated in Calcutta and at Harvard, while Duflo studied in Paris and at MIT. Today they jointly run the Abdul Latif Jameel Poverty Action Lab. Both are professors of economics at MIT.

Banerjee and Duflo are critical of both Easterly and Sachs—and Collier by implication. They say the debate cannot be solved by abstract arguments. Like Easterly, they favor running controlled experiments in poverty alleviation. They note there is always an anecdote available somewhere to prove someone's abstract position. So is there an answer to how to go about development?

> There are in fact answers—indeed, this whole book is in the form of an extended answer—it is just that they are not the kind of sweeping answers that Sachs and Easterly favor...
>
> More important, the endless debates about the rights and wrongs of aid often obscure what really matters: not so much where the money comes from, but where it goes...
>
> The natural place to start to unravel the mystery is to assume that the poor must know what they are doing. (Banerjee and Duflo 2011, 4–5, 25)

Thus they have engaged in worldwide grassroots research in eighteen countries, working from the base assumption that the poor have to work very hard—and work very smart—simply to survive. If they don't respond to our Western programs the way we want, they must have good reasons. And when they get a little extra cash, if they don't spend it how we would like, there must be good reasons for that too.

Banerjee and Duflo call into question many of the West's sweeping answers. For instance, they cast doubt on whether microfinance is a one-size-fits-all solution for the poor. They note that the overwhelming majority of poor people do not want to assume the risk and uncertainty of running their own farm or business; they are simply forced into it. They remind us the same is true of Westerners; the overwhelming majority of us would prefer a stable, good-paying job to being an entrepreneur.

So microfinance for micro-entrepreneurs may not be the sweeping solution some see it to be. It may be that the most pressing need is local jobs.

And just like Westerners, when the poor get a little extra money, they don't necessarily spend it all on more nutritious food. Just like us, they have a strong desire for a pleasant life. So they often spend extra money on parties, TVs, entertainment, festivals, weddings, alcohol, and tobacco. Just like us.

Banerjee and Duflo sound like Easterly when they argue for randomized control trials, modeled on pharmaceutical trials. Yet they reject Easterly's ideologically motivated diagnosis, which they see as too simplistic. They recommend that we behave like scientists, observe the poor carefully, and assume they know what they are doing. Banerjee and Duflo propose carefully designed interventions and policies to aid the poor in their development. Solutions will differ wildly across the world, depending on local context and conditions.

As a result, Banerjee and Duflo offer no sweeping conclusions. They reject "lazy, formulaic thinking" (272) and ask us to look closely at the families and communities of the poor—and above all, to listen to the poor themselves. Banerjee and Duflo note the need for simple, truthful communication, because the poor often have bad information. They also face too many daily choices, some of which could be simplified with better infrastructure. For instance, chlorinated water supplies preempt the financial decision on whether to purify the household's water or not, and they would dramatically reduce instances of waterborne disease. Banerjee and Duflo also recognize that cultural expectations will have to change—which can be done, though slowly. They call for empirical testing for any idea, project, or policy, no matter how commonsense it seems. They call for millions of local experiments to find out what works:

> We also have no lever guaranteed to eradicate poverty, but once we accept that, time is on our side. Poverty has been with us for many thousands of years; if we have to wait another fifty or hundred years for the end of poverty, so be it. At least we can stop pretending there is some solution at hand and instead join hands with millions of well-intentioned people across the world—elected officials and bureaucrats, teachers and NGO workers, academics and entrepreneurs—in the quest for many ideas, big and small, that will eventually take us to that world where no one has to live on 99 cents per day. (Banerjee and Duflo 2011, 273)

The other Global South perspective is *Just Give Money to the Poor: The Development Revolution from the Global South* by Joseph Hanlon, Armando Barrientos, and David Hulme. Though written by Westerners, the work documents an approach to development that is being carried out by developing countries themselves across the Global South, from Mexico to Indonesia, apart from Western aid projects or schemes. Over forty-five countries now give cash transfers directly to over 110 million poor families. Hanlon and his coauthors declare war early in the book:

> Aid has not failed; what has failed is an aid and anti-poverty industry that thrives on complexity

and mystification, with highly paid consultants designing ever more complicated projects for "the poor" and continuing to impose policy conditions on poor countries. This book offers the southern alternative: Give the money directly to those who have the least of it, but who know how to make the best use of it. Cash transfers are not charity or philanthropy but, rather, investments that enable poor people to take control of their own development and end their own poverty. Thus, this book is a direct challenge to Moyo, Collier, and much of the current popular writing on aid...

The southern response is a quiet revolution that has created a new development paradigm. It says that, rather than international sources giving aid to government bureaucrats and consultants, North and South, it should be given directly to poor people so they can pull themselves out of the poverty trap...

Of course, no one argues that all social spending or aid money should suddenly be given to poor people. Spending on health, education, infrastructure, and government itself remains essential. But without cash, poor people cannot make adequate use of these facilities. Thus giving money directly to poor people is just as important as spending on health and education. (Hanlon, Barrientos, and Hulme 2010, 8–11)

Their provocative thesis actually has interesting implications for a church-based approach to R&D. The apostle Paul's gift for the poor Jerusalem church was a "cash transfer" from the churches in his network. The authors of *Just Give Money to the Poor* are essentially recommending a similar tactic: bypass or ignore traditional Western aid agencies and government programs. Instead, the governments of poor countries themselves should be giving money directly to their poor citizens. This is usually called "welfare" in the United States. These governments of the Global South that are documented in Hanlon's book have discovered that small but reliable cash disbursements to the poorest of their citizens does in fact have a "bootstrapping" effect. The point of *Just Give Money to the Poor* is that the poorest don't even "have a boot to bootstrap!" This runs against popular assumptions in the United States that (1) welfare makes people lazy and dependent, and (2) it's their own fault for being poor in the first place. Hanlon and his cowriters make the case that these assumptions are simply wrong. We are blinded to the many infrastructural and institutional advantages we enjoy in the West. In the Global South, public opinion does not blame the poor themselves for being poor but instead blames unfair social and governmental structures. As for making the poor lazy, the authors document that this is generally not the case:

> That giving people money promotes laziness and dependency is one of the arguments most often advanced against cash transfers, yet it is proving to be a huge myth... Indeed, the evidence is that, at least on average, people work harder because the cash helps them out of the poverty trap. (Hanlon, Barrientos, and Hulme 2010, 73)

They continue by quoting Namibia Bishop Dr. Zephania Kameeta:

> Moreover, if you look in depth at Exodus 16, the people of Israel in the long journey out of slavery, they received manna from heaven. But it did not make them lazy; instead it enabled them to be on the move to travel through the desert. In Namibia, we know how harsh the circumstances of the desert can be. In this context nobody would say the manna made the Israelites dependent. To the contrary, it enabled them to move. (Hanlon, Barrientos, and Hulme 2010, 74)

This from authors who are very careful to base their proposal in "rights," not in biblical charity or alms! The authors believe there is a human right—granted by the United Nations—to a decent income. They do propose a role for the wealthy Global North: supplement or fund more cash transfers from governments in poor countries directly to their poorest citizens.

The United Nations' International Labour Organization "estimates that it would cost only 2 percent of global GDP to provide basic cash transfers for the world's poor" (Hanlon, Barrientos, and Hulme 2010, 155). They are referring to the nearly three billion people who live below the international poverty line of $2 a day. World military spending is 2.4 percent of global GDP (about $2.25 for every poor person), and the United States represents 42 percent of all military spending (Hanlon, Barrientos, and Hulme 2010, 155). Hanlon and his colleagues would like to see not more aid but increased transfers of cash from wealthy nations to the poor living in the poorest nations.

Further, "the initial response from the North was disbelief, and huge numbers of studies (on which this book is based) were commissioned. The studies showed that cash transfers work: They reduce both immediate and intergenerational poverty, and they stimulate the economy and promote development" (Hanlon, Barrientos and Hulme 2010, 167).

Their conclusions:

Cash transfers are not social programs that can wait until after development; instead, they are an essential precursor to growth and a driver of development...

Over the past decade, cash transfers have emerged as the response of the Global South to the need for economic development and poverty reduction. The northern-led extreme free market model of the 1980s and 1990s failed in the South, not only not bringing development but often leading to increased poverty and inequality...

The South has been rethinking the problem from the bottom up. Poor people, who have struggled to survive on tiny amounts of cash, are good economists who use additional money wisely...

The key is to trust poor people and directly give them cash. (Hanlon, Barrientos, and Hulme 2010, 175)

The proposal of their book aligns to some degree with the apostolic insistence on sharing among churches, which was noted in chapter two. Imagine the potential impact of cash transfers among international church networks, administered not by governments but by trustworthy church leaders!

When we turn to the evangelical literature, the most interesting perspectives once again come from voices in the Global South. Generally speaking, the North American evangelical literature tends to be much less ideological than the marketplace literature and is highly pragmatic in nature.

The evangelical literature is, of course, not concerned as much with the debate over large, top-down government aid programs. It tends to focus on smaller projects, but this does not necessarily imply a bottom-up orientation. Indeed, nearly all the North American evangelical literature evidences a "West knows best for the rest" mentality. Here's one example:

> Developing nations are looking to the West to teach them the principles and skills for successful business... More important than teaching business principles, we must equip the nations with the transforming power of the gospel, which leads to growth of their spiritual capital. Spiritual capital is the base on which successful businesses must be built. We cannot shortchange developing economies by exporting the capitalist system without the foundation that made it thrive in the West—the biblical values that permeated the culture and grew spiritual capital. (Eldred 2009, 115)

World Vision and Compassion International are two very large R&D evangelical organizations. *The Hole in Our Gospel* from World Vision and *Fast Living* from Compassion are both impassioned presentations of the need for R&D. Both appeal for increased awareness of global poverty, increased giving on the part of US Christians and churches, increased advocacy with governments on behalf of the poor, and increased mobilization of US Christians in observation or vision trips and child sponsorship. Both organizations cooperate with local churches and organization, but the overall mind-set is one of large projects (for evangelicals, anyway) funded by the West.

As noted above, there is a growing awareness—perhaps even a consensus—that the millions of dollars spent by US Christians on short-term mission trips are grossly ineffective for development (Corbett and Fikkert 2009, 161–179). While these trips may be helpful during the relief phase of a crisis, they do not help much with development. There are several voices calling for money to simply be given to local people on the ground or used to hire local labor for development projects. Peter Greer, author of *The Poor Will Be Glad*, made a presentation during the Rebuild Haiti track at the 2012 Movement Day in New York City, in which he called for the complete cessation of short-term trips so that churches could invest instead in microfinance or business development solutions. The idea is good in theory but often fails in practice. An American Christian will raise several thousand dollars to travel to a distant country. That same Christian might be reluctant to simply write a check for the same amount and give it to an unknown and disconnected church or some other organization. Nevertheless, there is a growing consensus—as evidenced by books like *When Helping Hurts, The Poor Will Be Glad, Toxic Charity*, and others—that the evangelical short-term mission trip "industry" needs to be rethought.

The evangelical literature coming out of the business-as-mission (BAM) movement, on the other hand, is another story. First, a definition of BAM:

> BAM generally means a for-profit business which is formed specifically to demonstrate Christian principles and practices to employees, customers, and suppliers and to improve the income and infrastructures of the surrounding community—all to the greater glory of God. (Greer and Smith 2009, 227)

As different versions of "free market capitalism" expand around the globe, fueled by the success of India and China, a growing number of evangelical development efforts are hitching a ride. There is not yet much actual conversation in the literature about this development. One can find a variety of statements regarding the potential of BAM. Beyond the literature being reviewed are statements from recent Lausanne conferences, for instance (Lausanne 2004). But there has not been much interaction among the various authors and organizations. There does seem to be some consensus developing around the following ideas:

- Business is a kingdom vocation just as is pastoring or traditional missionary work.

> [The business owners] came to see that R&D workers often looked at poverty through the

lenses of social sciences rather than business. As a result, their focus tended to be on meeting the immediate basic needs (a good thing!), but not on broader economic sustainability… The revolutionary message needed to be delivered emphatically and unapologetically: business is not just business; in reality it is an outstanding Christian calling. (Seebeck and Stoner 2009, 30–31)

- BAM has a direct, not indirect, impact on the economies of developing countries and is therefore more effective in development work than many—if not all—NGOs and short-term trips.

  [Partners Worldwide's] model differs significantly from that of the conventional short-term mission trips. There has been much written lately about the cost benefit of such missional ventures… Our partners, rather than doing a building project and leaving the country for good, work on strategic, long-term partnerships that build capacity, businesses, leadership and talent to create sustainable jobs far into the future. (Seebeck and Stoner 2009, 79–80)

- People the world over are interested in owning their own business or having a good job. However, the obstacles they face are overwhelming. US businesspeople and companies are perfectly positioned to help them overcome these obstacles. Kingdom business is for-profit business ventures designed to facilitate God's transformation of people and nations. (Eldred 2009, 60)

- Microfinancing of impoverished entrepreneurs is a major opportunity for business development.
- Mentoring, resourcing, and consulting with existing small businesses in an impoverished country can be a great opportunity for job creation.
- Direct capital investment in local businesses by US-based investors is a third major opportunity.
- These BAM initiatives should be conducted with kingdom ethics, with evangelism as a high priority, and they should support the local church.

The current overriding need in developing nations is for economic development, and Kingdom business professionals are a welcome solution. Consider the following observations... Free market capitalism is the most powerful economic force in the world today... Investment has soundly overtaken aid as the preferred method for assisting developing countries...

God desires to bless the nations spiritually and physically. It stands to reason that He will use the current trends toward capitalism and economic development to further the establishment of His Kingdom. (Eldred 2009, 47–48)

This emphasis on business as life work, on marketplace vocation, is very welcome. Although this conversation is young in evangelicalism, it has great potential. It must be said, however, that much of the theological reflection in this literature is superficial at best. Going forward, there are several areas that need to be addressed by the BAM movement and its literature:

- Colonialism and its aftereffects. There is a naive reading of history in some of this literature about the spread of evangelicalism around the world in conjunction with the spread of western imperialism in the nineteenth and twentieth centuries.

- Individualism. A lot of the BAM material reflects an individualistic understanding of salvation and appeals to an individual's sense of responsibility. While almost all this literature tips the hat to the church, there seems to be little recognition of the church as a countercultural society with its own distinct economics—distinct even from American capitalism.

- Utilitarianism. In some instances, the case is made that Christianity is helpful to the spread of capitalism, because of Christian ethics and the culture-formation potential of the church. This type of argument puts capitalism, rather than the kingdom of God, in the driver's seat as the hope of the world. The church becomes a helpful secondary institution in this model.

- Capitalism. Occasionally advocates of BAM will acknowledge the tension between Jesus' and his apostles' teaching on money on the one hand, and the driving assumptions of capitalism on the other. In many cases, though, the tenets of capitalism are assumed to be in complete harmony with the Bible:

> If there is one principle that underlies the economic system of capitalism, it is the notion of inalienable property rights. This involves the intrinsic right to own, control and use private property . . .
>
> ...Unlike the modern examples of socialism, capitalism rests on the biblical principle of personal freedom and responsibility. Man is free to use his gifts in the manner in which he chooses . . .
>
> In the Old Testament, God's people owned private land, animals and money. It was a "capitalist" system. The Israelites were free to do with their property as they chose [except sell it]... In essence, the Old Testament depicts free enterprise with a somewhat illiquid real estate market. (Eldred 2009, 76)

Overwhelmingly this literature works off the assumption that capitalism is good and good for us, offering almost no biblical correction or critique. Eldred quotes, with approval, Dr. David Livingstone's colonial-era 150-year-old comment, "Those two pioneers of civilization—Christianity and commerce—should ever be inseparable" (Eldred 2009, 42).

What is needed is a robust biblical theology to inform the BAM conversation. In particular, BAM proponents would do well to draw from two recent works, which represent some of the best theological thinking currently available: *Walking with the Poor*, a Western book that relies heavily on sources and missiology from the Global South, and *God of the Empty-Handed*, an even more foundational work from an Indian theologian. Their contribution will be reviewed in the following section.

Top down or bottom up? While there is not as strong a consensus on this question as there is on the critique of past R&D efforts, there is growing momentum on the side of smaller, grassroots initiatives—local initiatives rooted in a particular culture, a particular land, a particular people. This also represents an enormous opportunity for a truly "local theology" approach to R&D. As the gospel "seed" is planted in local soil, it can grow its own kingdom solutions that are best suited for that community's very particular time and place.

## 3. Guilty Secret: The Role of Values, Religion, and Culture

For some time, it was unacceptable to talk about culture and cultural values as possible contributors to poverty and obstacles to economic development. Mindful of racist and imperialist attitudes from a previous era, the marketplace literature stayed away from this topic.

In the 1940s and 1950s, much attention was paid to culture as a crucial element in understanding societies, analyzing differences among them, and explaining their economic and political development... work on culture in the academic community declined dramatically in the 1960s and 1970s. Then, in the 1980s, interest in culture as an explanatory variable began to revive...

...In the scholarly world, the battle has thus been joined by those who see culture as a major, but not the only, influence on social, political, and economic behavior and those who adhere to universal explanations. (Harrison and Huntington 2000, xiii–xiv)

The long-accepted academic dogma assumed that a combination of colonialism and dependency were the "universal explanations" for countries trapped in poverty. However, there is an emerging body of literature from both the Global North and South that asserts that the shelf life for these as all-encompassing explanations is running short:

A growing number of scholars, journalists, politicians, and development practitioners are focusing on the role of cultural values and attitudes as facilitators of, or obstacles to, progress. (Harrison and Huntington 2000, xxi)

Without a doubt, cultures around the globe have been affected by colonialism and dependency. In fact, the colonizers, dependency-creators, and their cultures were negatively affected as well. So the move to include additional cultural factors in our understanding of economic development should not be seen as dismissing these harmful effects. The reasons for poverty are complex. For too long, however, cultural values were not discussed as possible contributors to poverty. Today there is a growing awareness that cultural and religious values must be considered, along with outside influences like colonialism.

This growing view is still resisted, notably by Jeffrey Sachs, whose work continues to set much of the agenda in marketplace literature. Sachs does not dispute that there can be cultural values and norms that contribute to poverty. His concern is that such observations have sometimes been used to dismiss all efforts at aid and change. The idea that certain cultures are and always will be black holes of aid, that corruption is an intractable part of some cultures and can't be altered, that morals are so low in some countries that there's no way to stem the tide of HIV and AIDS—these beliefs, Sachs says, are simply incorrect.

> [They represent] conventional rich-world wisdom about Africa, and to a lesser extent, other poor regions. While common, these assertions are incorrect. Yet they have been repeated publicly for so long, or whispered in private, that they have become accepted as truths by the broad public as well as much of the development community. (Sachs 2005, 309)

Sachs points out that early in the twentieth century, cultural analysis was used to demonstrate that Confucian-based societies in Asia could never develop as Christian-based societies of the West had. Later, when China and other Asian countries began to grow, credit was given to Asian values, "turning the argument on its head" (316). At the same time, Sachs acknowledges the fact that certain cultural beliefs and values do impede economic development:

> Even when governments are trying to advance their countries, the cultural environment may

be an obstacle to development. Cultural or religious norms in the society may block the role of women, for example, leaving half of the population without economic or political rights and without education, thereby undermining half of the population in its contribution to overall development. (Sachs 2005, 60)

So there seems to be an emerging consensus that culture can play a role in causing poverty or impeding development, though there is ongoing debate on how large a role it plays. Perhaps a more ticklish subject is the question of "culture change." If culture plays some role in poverty, at what point (and to what extent) is it appropriate to pursue "culture change" in the name of poverty reduction? Some in the conversation view any effort to change a culture as imperialism, imposing a Western view of progress on cultures that have a different understanding of the good life. In extreme cases, cultural relativists argue that we have no right to criticize a culture's treatment of women—say, genital mutilation or immolation of widows—or even their practice of slavery (Harrison and Huntington 2000, xxvi).

A symposium was held at the Harvard Academy for International and Area Studies in 1999 to address these questions.

One of the most controversial issues debated at the symposium, an issue that dominated the wrap-up session, was the extent to which cultural change should be integrated into the conceptualizing, strategizing, planning, and programming of political and economic development...

> ...Few [past] interventions were designed to promote cultural change, and indeed the whole idea of promoting cultural change has been taboo. (Harrison and Huntington 2000, xxx)

The idea that culture change must be a part of poverty alleviation—a school of thought that includes Westerners, Africans, and Latin American scholars—is represented by *Culture Matters*, which summarizes its position as follows:

> If some cultural values are fundamental obstacles to progress—if they help explain the intractability of the problems of poverty and injustice in a good part of the Third World—then there is no alternative to the promotion of cultural change. It need not, indeed should not, be viewed as a Western imposition. (Harrison and Huntington 2000, xxxi)

This from an African contributor:

> If Europe, that fragment of earth representing a tiny part of humanity, has been able to impose itself on the planet, dominating it and organizing it for its exclusive profit, it is only because it developed a conquering culture of rigor and work, *removed from the influence of invisible forces.* We must do the same. (Etounga-Manguelle in Harrison and Huntington 2000, 77, emphasis added)

The solutions offered in the essays of *Culture Matters* are intensely secular. While the role of religion is certainly an important part of culture, the proposed solutions move beyond religion, which Etounga-Manguelle styles above as "influence of invisible forces" or as "blind submission to the irrational" (77). In the final essay, Lawrence Harrison—perhaps the leader in the revival of cultural explanations for poverty—offers ten "mind-sets that distinguish progressive cultures from static cultures":

1. Time orientation—awareness of a future, belief in the ability to influence destiny
2. Work as central to the good life, not a burden
3. Frugality as the "mother of investment"
4. A commitment to education for everyone
5. The importance of merit counts, not social connections or family status
6. A sense of community—and trust—that extends beyond the family to broader society
7. Rigorous ethical code
8. Justice and fair play as impersonal forces, not influenced by one's connections
9. Decentralized authority
10. Secularism—namely, that "the influence of religious institution on civic life is small" (Harrison and Huntington 200, 299–300)

Reviewing these "ten commandments" of culture change, it's obvious that several are highly compatible with a biblical theology and Christian worldview, and in fact have their roots in biblical teaching. It's also obvious that Harrison does not regard faith or faith-based initiatives as part of the solution. We'll return to this issue in the last section of the chapter.

The concept of culture change—the idea that values, worldviews, mind-sets, and religions could contribute both to causing poverty and to overcoming poverty— is of course the home field of biblical religion. The goal of the gospel message is transformation—of individuals, households, households of households, and whole societies and cultures. Salt and light, leaven in the dough, shining like stars, city set on a hill, and on and on go the biblical metaphors for the influence of God's people toward culture change—culminating in the consummation or full arrival of the kingdom of God, the ultimate "culture change."

This is one reason for the recent explosion of evangelical interest in what used to be called "social action." Evangelicals have gotten over the false dichotomy of "evangelism versus social action":

> Over half of the incoming master's students to the School of Intercultural Studies at Fuller Theological Seminary in 2009 enrolled to study international development, children at risk, and urban ministry (Myers 2011, 49).

The explosion of short-term mission trips hasn't slowed down in spite of criticism, and small US-based evangelical NGOs continue to proliferate. Yet this is as good a place as any to note what is *not* happening:

> This is all well and good, but it is important to say what has *not* happened in evangelical thinking about development. No case studies have been published in the last ten years. There are very few serious evaluations that are genuinely holistic. There is very little, if any, serious research by Christian practitioners—very few Ph.D. studies and almost no evidence-based research into transformational development...

...We seem to be resting on the theological work done in the 1980s. We have a biblical and theological rationale for doing evangelism and social action, but almost nothing has been done theologically on how this transformational work might be done. (Myers 2011, 49)

Myers is a professor at Fuller and has served World Vision as a program advisor. His book *Walking with the Poor* is the most comprehensive evangelical publication on development to date. His subtitle—*Principles and Practices of Transformational Development*—tells you what he thinks about seeking cultural change. Though written by a Westerner, he depends heavily on several Global South theologians and development practitioners; Ravi Jayakaran, Jayakumar Christian, Nora Avarientos, and Sarone Ole Sena are particularly important. Jayakumar Christian's *God of the Empty-Handed* is the finest book I've found yet on kingdom theology and poverty. The subtitle is telling: *Poverty, Power and the Kingdom of God*.

In addition, Myers draws heavily on Paul Hiebert's missiological work on the "excluded middle" of Western cultures and its importance in understanding traditional cultures. The "excluded middle" is a phrase Hiebert uses to refer to the Western mind-set that there is a high God of formal religion and a physical realm where everything can be explained by natural causes. Supernatural beings or activities are excluded from the natural realm. However, in traditional cultures (like ancient Israel), the activities of angels, demons, leprechauns, magicians, and wizards are all included as part of a middle, informal religion. Myers notes that most development practitioners are most comfortable in the natural world, and so they miss the role of the middle realm in the culture they're attempting to help develop (Myers 2011, 209).

Myers and Christian, taken together, provide the best current theological foundation for thinking about R&D, and in particular the issue of culture change and how it comes about. Christian's work is the more foundational of the two, and he has this to say about Jesus' gospel of the kingdom:

> Jesus was interested in politics. He challenged the political structures by challenging the meaning of political relationships and the way power and leadership were exercised. Jesus' whole life and relationships were different from all other militant groups... Jesus called society to live with a different frame of reference—the kingdom of God. Rather than heed his call, we preferred to kill him. (Christian 1999, 173)

Christian emphasizes the powerlessness of the poor. He proposes that poverty eradication must deal with the issues of power and powerlessness. In particular, Christian demonstrates (biblically and anecdotally) how the powerlessness of poverty mars the image of God in the poor. Created to be powerful cocreators with God and made in his image so they can reign over God's creation in God's way, the poor now find themselves less than human, powerless in their cultural relationships of economics, politics, and social hierarchies.

Myers consciously adopts Christian's view, and he wants to add to it the role of vocation in restoring the full image of God in the poor, bringing together both being and doing in a restored humanity:

> To Jayakumar's proposal that transformation is the work of helping the poor recover their true identity as made in the image of God, I add the idea that vocation or calling is also part of true identity. Our identity in biblical terms is both who we are and what we do. (Myers 2011, xxiv)

These two authors give a well-thought-out and biblically grounded answer to the following question: Is culture part of the poverty problem and is intentional culture change appropriate in poverty alleviation? "Development by definition is about changing culture and changing culture is about changing values and worldviews" (Myers 2011, 350). This whole area of culture and development should be one to which Christians make great contributions. The last part of this chapter will seek to give a partial answer to the "how" of cultural transformation.

But first this perhaps obvious observation: the reentry of religion and culture change into the R&D conversation represents an enormous opportunity for the church and its theologians and leaders. Has a better strategy for positive cultural change than that of Christ and his apostles ever been imagined? The spontaneous expansion of the kingdom for 300 years through the establishing of new "Jesus communities"—Kingdom Outposts—throughout the Roman Empire changed Western civilization forever. While it was not a quick solution, it was a profound and permanent cultural change for the better. The successful implementation of the way of Christ and his apostles stands today as the most profound example of culture change in human history.

## 4. The Invisible Church

The phrase *invisible church* is used to describe the Christian movement as God sees it—true believers, scattered throughout all denominations and expressions of Christianity, and perhaps even outside of formal association with Christianity. I'd like to use it here in a different sense: the church is largely "invisible" in the R&D literature. This is not to say that one cannot find references to the church as a whole and to local churches scattered through the evangelical literature and occasionally in the marketplace literature. But the church is largely invisible—even in the Christian literature—as a serious answer to the "how" of doing effective poverty alleviation and economic development.

Not that religion is invisible. Peter Berger framed this up well nearly forty years ago:

> Development is not just a goal of rational actions in the economic, political and social spheres. It is also, and very deeply, the focus of redemptive hopes and expectations. In an important sense, *development is a religious category...* Unless this is understood, much of what is taking place in the Third World today will remain incomprehensible... The myth of growth, and indeed the entire mythology of modernity, derives from the specifically Western tradition of messianism. *Ultimately, it represents a secularization of*

*biblical eschatology...* Its success as a new
"gospel" has been enormous. As a result of this,
whoever speaks of economic growth in the Third
World today is not just engaging in economics,
but is rousing a whole array of redemptive
aspirations, the ultimate content of which is
mythic. It is this content that provides much
of the power to sway, inspire, mobilize—and,
if frustrated, to enrage. (Berger 1976, 17, 19,
emphasis added)

This is a remarkable statement. If accurate—and I
think it is—it confirms the theology I summarized in
chapter two. R&D is a major part of salvation. However,
R&D as usually studied and practiced is an alternative
salvation to the way of Christ. Much of the secular
literature has a religious fervor to it and does indeed
represent "a secularization of biblical eschatology."
There is a vision for what Jesus calls the "kingdom
of God"—without the God! It is an evangelism of a
"new gospel."

In *Just Give Money to the Poor*, the authors quote
Deuteronomy at the beginning of a chapter entitled
"From Alms to Rights and North to South":

Helping poor people is one of the fundamental
duties prescribed in all of the world's major
religions. In a phrase probably written in the
7th century BCE, the Jewish Torah and Christian
Bible (Deuteronomy 15:11) say that "[there will
never cease to be poor in the land. Therefore I
command you, 'You shall open wide your hand

to your brother, to the needy and to the poor, in your land].' " . . .

. . . Over the centuries, production systems and our attitudes have slowly changed. Our "land" has become the entire world, and we no longer accept that the poor will always be with us. Ending poverty has become a global goal. (Hanlon, Barrientos, and Hulme 2010, 15)

In Hanlon's understanding, alms for the poor rooted in a divine command has given way to viewing income as a basic right rooted in a United Nations resolution. This is regarded as a correction of religion's misguided notion that there's nothing we can do about poverty except give charity. Secularization indeed.

Perhaps a better term than *secularization* is *desacralization*. As Berger points out above, "Development is a religious category." And if our biblical religion has an agrarian perspective, then we see our life as a gift from God to be nurtured, not as a right granted by a human institution. The primary reason the church is invisible in the marketplace literature is that the authors hold a desacralized view of the world. For from a Christian agrarian perspective, the world is not divided into sacred and secular; it is divided into sacred and desecrated. A worldview that sees the world as one big mine or one big factory or one big business is a desecrated worldview. Too much of the evangelical literature reviewed in this chapter also shares a desecrated economic worldview.

This is seen particularly when US evangelicals simply parrot the ideas of free-market capitalism. When we assume that all we need is a level playing field and that competition and enlightened self-interest will sort out the problems of poverty, we are preaching a "new gospel" as Berger said.

> The ideal of competition always implies, and in fact requires, that any community must be divided into a class of winners and a class of losers. This division is radically different from other social divisions: that of the more able and the less able or that of the richer and the poorer, or even that of the rulers and the ruled. These latter divisions have existed throughout history and at times, at least, have been ameliorated by social and religious ideals that instructed the strong to help the weak. As a purely economic ideal, competition does not contain or imply any such instructions. In fact, the defenders of the ideal of competition have never known what to do with or for the losers. The losers simply accumulate in human dumps, like stores of industrial waste, until they gain enough misery and strength to overpower the winners. (Berry 2010, 130–131)

Much of the influential marketplace literature excludes religion and/or the church specifically. *Helping People Help Themselves*, *The Bottom Billion*, *Dead Aid*, and *Poor Economics* simply don't address the topic. In fact, two of the most influential voices are visibly nervous about religion in general and American evangelicals in particular. Here's Easterly:

> Discussion of African beliefs in witchcraft is taboo in aid agencies, as nobody wants to reinforce ill-informed stereotypes. Unfortunately, political correctness gets in the way of making policy, as

conventional public health approaches may not work if people *do* believe that witchcraft causes illness and turn to traditional healers. Americans and Europeans also believed in witches when they were at similar levels of income as Africa (and many Americans still do today; hence the spiritualism section at the Barnes & Noble bookstore in Greenwich Village—one of the intellectual capitals of the United States—is three times the size of the science section). Moreover, many American evangelicals believe divine intervention can cure illness. (Easterly 2006, 248)

Jeffrey Sachs is more than nervous. He is terrified of certain American evangelicals:

The third fallacy is the "clash of civilizations," the belief that the world is entering a war of cultures. For many in America this is a literal war, the war of Armageddon. Millions of Americans, though just how many is unclear, believe that we are approaching the "end days" of biblical prophecy. This millennial belief has returned in waves in American history, but never before with the United States as a nuclear and global superpower. It is terrifying for those of us who would rather use rationality than scriptural prophecy to determine U.S. foreign policy. (Sachs 2005, 331)

Sachs was also nervous about some evangelicals' direct influence on the White House:

As the United States invaded Iraq and Afghanistan, millions of U.S. fundamentalist

Christians debated whether the rise of terrorism and Middle East conflict marked the end days of prophecy. The fictional *Left Behind* series of novels based on fundamentalist prophecy has sold tens of millions of volumes dramatizing a future Armageddon. Believers in these doctrines formed a powerful constituency within the Bush political coalition. If American foreign policy falls under the sway not only of unilateralism, or misconceived neoimperialism, but also irrational biblical prophecy as well, the risks for the world will multiply profoundly. (Sachs 2005, 360)

To counter this irrational fundamentalist influence in America, Sachs proposes a conscious return to secular Enlightenment convictions:

A fourth overarching Enlightenment vision joins Jefferson's vision of human-made political systems, Smith's rationally designed economic systems, and Kant's global arrangements for perpetual peace: that science and technology, fueled by human reason, can be a sustained force for social improvements and human betterment. (Sachs 2005, 349)

As Sachs wraps up his highly influential book, he reaches for three inspiring examples of his proposed Enlightened Globalization: the end of slavery in Britain and Europe in the early nineteenth century, championed by William Wilberforce; the end of colonialism nearly one hundred years later, inspired by Ghandi in India; and more recently the Civil Rights movement in the United States led by Dr. Martin Luther King Jr.

He asserts that these movements share "some basic features," that "they called upon fundamental Enlightenment values of human rights and human potentialities" (Sachs 2005, 364).

This assertion opens up an opportunity for Christians to fruitfully engage in the conversation and demonstrate the gospel of the kingdom. Sachs neglects to mention all three of his heroes were deeply religious. Wilberforce was a British evangelical Christian; Ghandi was a devout Hindu; and King was a passionate African American Christian. All three men were rooted not in Enlightenment values but in kingdom values. Two of the three were deeply rooted in Christian teaching and culture. I believe all three would agree with Sachs's concluding sentence: "Let the future say of our generation that we sent forth mighty currents of hope, and that we worked together to heal the world" (Sachs 2005, 368). But currents from what source?

As we turn to the evangelical literature on poverty alleviation, it's important to note that none of the authors reviewed in the next few paragraphs are opposed to the church. All of them heartily embrace the conviction that the church is God's idea, his plan, that it was founded by Jesus himself, and that he intends to grow it in number, maturity, and influence. All of them think the church is important, even indispensable. Their doctrine of the church, rooted usually in a systematic theology approach, is completely orthodox.

This clarification is necessary in order to offer a critique of the evangelical understanding of the church's role in poverty alleviation and economic development. As we will see, even in some evangelical literature, the "invisible church" is the only one you'll find. Others issue a stirring cry for more financial involvement from churches, but when it comes to actually delivering development, they do not include the church. Others include the church, but only as an outside resource, partner, or ally to development professionals who are driving the process and programs. With one or two shining exceptions, the theological perspective of this thesis—that the local church (and its network) is the actual locus of R&D work and that this work of salvation is spread by the founding of Kingdom Outposts—is not represented in the literature.

The BAM literature evidences both a frustration with and allegiance to church. The purpose of Seebeck's book *My Business, My Mission* is to present the work of Partners Worldwide, which serves to connect US business mentors with emerging international small businesses in over eighteen countries, for the purpose of job creation. Partners Worldwide has a firm Reformed theological base, including its view of the church. But the local church is almost entirely absent from *My Business, My Mission*. Here is one comment, based on the observation of a Haitian Christian businessman:

> Ernso tells us that his call and the call of others like him is to change Haiti not only with the gospel, but with business. He observes that missionaries have done a marvelous job of personal conversion (over 60% of the population claim to be Christian) but have had virtually no impact on society. Haiti, the country with the largest number of converts in the Western Hemisphere, is also one of the

poorest countries. I agree with Ernso's point. When conversion of millions makes no impact on a society, other than the construction of an inordinate number of church buildings, there is something very troubling going on. (Seebeck and Stoner 2009, 124)

Ernso goes on to proclaim that through business the gospel will spread in Haiti and that through the poverty reduction that business achieves, Jesus will be honored. This is a great illustration of what deeply concerns me about the BAM literature. Like Seebeck, I agree wholeheartedly with Ernso's observation. There is indeed something very troubling going on in Haiti and elsewhere. However, when you have millions of converts who in turn have had "virtually no impact on society," before we abandon ship on local churches, we should be asking hard questions. What's wrong with the gospel we've been proclaiming? And therefore what's wrong with our understanding of a local church? Why would Ernso see business as something in addition to, or outside of, the gospel? Biblically, is the work of missionaries defined as obtaining personal conversions? What is wrong with our definition of salvation if it does not include poverty eradication?

But instead of asking these questions, in works like Eldred's *God Is at Work*, we get a reduced understanding of mission as personal evangelism combined with an assumption that business is the best vehicle for meeting people's needs:

The concept of Kingdom business sees business as missions. It considers business activity itself the missions work. Kingdom businesses are for-profit businesses that meet spiritual, social and economic needs…

…By speaking truth and living out their faith in the workplace, they are able to lead many to Christ… Kingdom business is missions. (Eldred 2009, 72–73)

It doesn't sound like there is much left for a church to do. That being said, the local church is not absent from Eldred's work. In fact, supporting the local church is one of the three objectives of a kingdom business. Eldred devotes an entire section of his book to "Advancing the Local Church and Building Spiritual Capital." He sums up this idea as follows:

*Potential measures of success.* The local church may be advanced by adding to its numbers, by improving its standing in the community, and by increasing its economic resources. (Eldred 2009, 163)

Interestingly, Eldred never spells out his understanding of the actual mission of a local church. In his enthusiasm for kingdom business, it often sounds as if the local church is not needed at all.

Democracy is not a prerequisite for Kingdom business; nor is establishment of democracies the objective of Kingdom business—the objective is to bring the gospel of Christ and see lives radically transformed by the power of the Holy Spirit. We must simultaneously bring business and the truth of Christ in the Spirit of God. (Eldred 2009, 133)

Kingdom business professionals are best equipped to bring the transforming gospel that leads to spiritual capital. (Eldred 2009, 179)

At the same time, Eldred is genuinely excited about the possibility of church planting:

*Kingdom business is credited with starting 10,000 new churches around the world.* As people come to Jesus, churches will spring up. (Eldred 2009, 262)

I'm actually greatly encouraged by the BAM movement. But the theological underpinnings are weak, and this leads to a mishmash of convictions about business and church that make mistaken assumptions about mission, church, and the kingdom.

Dr. Brian Fikkert's very popular *When Helping Hurts* is an accessible introduction to the issues of R&D and is well grounded in a sophisticated Reformed theology of work, the image of God, sin, and salvation. He seems to see the local church as an indispensable partner in poverty reduction, particularly entrusted with the verbal proclamation of the gospel:

This implies that the local church, as an institution, has a key role to play in poverty alleviation, because the gospel has been committed by God to the church. This does *not* mean that the local church must own, operate, and manage all ministries. Parachurch ministries and individuals have a role to play as well. However, it does mean that we cannot hope for the transformation of people without the involvement of the local church and the verbal proclamation of the gospel that has been entrusted to it. (Corbett and Fikkert 2009, 81)

Specifically, Fikkert sees that the local church has a role to play in proclaiming a gospel that has a vision for changing all of life, including material poverty:

> Churches are uniquely positioned to provide the relational ministries on an individual level that people like Alisa need...
>
> ...[C]hurches can also offer Alisa something that [her employer] could not: a clear articulation of the gospel of the kingdom so that Alisa can experience the profound and lasting change required to achieve material poverty alleviation in its fullest sense: *the ability to fulfill her calling of glorifying God through her work and life.* (Corbett and Fikkert 2009, 97)

Richard Stearns, president of World Vision U.S., has written a stirring call to action in *The Hole in Our Gospel*. Throughout the book he names the enormous potential of the American church for poverty alleviation, noting the number of Christians, the number of congregations, their current giving, and their enormous wealth and untapped giving potential. He cites the example of the early church and its widespread influence on the Roman Empire and the daily life of that society, calling it a "social revolution" spread by the new communities of Jesus:

> After the Resurrection, we read that Jesus' disciples became such incredible agents of change that they literally altered the course of history. The communities they started and the values they

practiced were so striking to the world around them that they ignited a social revolution that drew thousands and ultimately billions to faith in Christ. (Stearns 2009, 244)

Yet when it comes time to ask the question of "what to do?" the answers are individualistic and focused on the parachurch. We should give more money. World Vision is a trusted R&D organization that does value local churches:

In Christian-majority contexts, where our witness can be fully expressed, we work to meet people's material needs and encourage spiritual maturity—for example, we partner with local churches to provide opportunities for children and families to experience life in Christ. (Stearns 2009, 302)

But there is almost nothing said about the role of local churches in poor countries in poverty alleviation. And the role of local churches in the United States seems primarily one of economic support—not directly supporting churches and church networks in the manner of Paul's collection for the Jerusalem church, but rather US churches being challenged to financially support Christian R&D organizations.

An even more church-centered call for action comes from Scott Todd, Senior Ministry Advisor for Compassion International, and his book *Fast Living: How the Church Will End Extreme Poverty*. His goal is the end of extreme poverty, defined as people trying to survive on $1.25 a day or less. As his subtitle suggests, Todd sees the church as the means to this end, in partnership with development organizations:

> The Christian development organization should focus on serving one aspect of the Church's mission—helping the most vulnerable meet their basic needs. That work should be integrated with making disciples and is part of the journey toward human flourishing (shalom). But development organizations should focus on the enormous task of lifting people out of economic poverty and into a state of sufficiency. The rest of the journey toward shalom, the journey we are all on, is for the Church to nurture. (Todd 2011, 85)

Todd sees culture as divided into three key sectors: government, business, and the social sector, the last of which includes churches and parachurch organizations. He believes that both government and business have a huge role to play in eradicating poverty. And he calls on the church to advocate with governments on behalf of the poor, and for American Christians to use our mind-boggling wealth to support fair trade and cause-based businesses. But he proposes the church as the ultimate answer. He notes the church's "strategic assets," like the millions of change agents the church deploys into a society, or the "service delivery points" (local churches) dispersed around the globe. And then he makes this very clear statement:

> The ultimate reason why the Church is critical to the work of ending poverty is the promise of Jesus. Jesus was given the government option and declined. Jesus could have started a business for

social good, but he didn't. Instead he established the Church and promised that "the gates of hell shall not prevail against it" (Matthew 16:18 [ESV]). The Church, expressed in local disciple-making communities, is commissioned by Jesus and empowered by the Holy Spirit to advance the Kingdom on earth. And that advance includes the eradication of the evil of extreme poverty. (Todd 2011, 150)

This is the finest theological statement in the literature reviewed so far. However, when Todd turns to strategic implementation, he offers vague and individualistic solutions. "Church" seems to be conceived of as an amalgamation of Christian individuals. There seems to be little developed understanding of "church" as firmly established alternative local communities, functioning as extended households of God. Todd suggests that American Christians should commit to giving a full 10 percent tithe specifically to poverty reduction. We should involve our young people in hands-on service projects to give them a compelling vision on how to spend their money and their lives. Christians should advocate for the poor and utilize consumerism to influence business toward poverty alleviation. Like Stearns, there is much to admire and agree with in Todd's writing. But neither seems to know what to do with impoverished local churches in the developing world—nor with wealthy US churches other than receive their financial support.

The most robust, practical suggestions for partnering with the church are found in Greer's *The Poor Will Be Glad*. Both the local church and networks of churches feature prominently in his proposals for poverty eradication. He would like to see several development strategies integrated into local churches that minister in poor settings—strategies and programs like savings and credit associations (SCAs), business training, microfinance accountability groups, pastoral training (so pastors can in turn train their congregations on how to use increasing wealth), and partnerships with organizations like his own Hope International. Greer says that microfinance organizations like Hope International represent the "second-best distribution system for poor people in the world." As for the best?

> The church is the best distribution system in the world...
>
> ...[T]he church has far greater scope and scale than virtually any other social entity.
>
> Besides being widespread, local church leadership in other countries often has much more influence over the lives of their church members than would leadership in an American church where individuality is so highly prized...
>
> Churches around the world are often the most influential distribution systems in their communities. Savvy governments and aid groups have long known this and use the influence of churches whenever feasible. (Greer and Smith 2009, 155–157)

The recognition that the church is "the best distribution system in the world" is most welcome and accords with the idea of financial sharing in church networks. Not as welcome is the utilitarian view that many "governments and aid groups" have of local churches.

This is exactly why the church is uniquely qualified to engage in economic development. The church has the moral resources to transform hearts as it improves incomes. This combination is the only way that significant and lasting societal change is possible. (Greer and Smith 2009, 171)

Throughout his book, Greer calls on outside development organizations to partner closely with the local churches. He calls it "the most obvious and beneficial resource available" (197). He goes on to say,

Within this partnership, the indigenous local church must be central... The local church has not been intimately involved in many Christian development projects around the world, much to the detriment of the local church—and to the detriment of the projects. Working with the local church is not easy, yet this church is, and always will be, Christ's body on earth to whom he entrusts the task of feeding the poor and clothing the naked. (Greer and Smith 2009, 254)

And here is the fly in the ointment. The local church is "not easy" to work with. Many organizations would say this is the understatement of the year. The highly utilitarian view that the church can be "used" effectively by aid agencies runs smack into the independence and immaturity of many churches, to name just two issues. Many international churches and networks are also infected with the same industrial view of the world that we have exported from the West—or a desacralized understanding of the world and its economics. Many still suffer from the theological split between evangelism and social action that plagued the US church for years. The same power that makes local pastors such a strong influence also gives them the ability to block or kill an initiative from the outside. While I have found this to be a widespread view held by many, Greer does us the service of naming it and putting his finger on the issue:

> A common hindrance to working with the local church is the lack of reliable local leadership. Sometimes the solution, rather than turning away, is to raise up and train local leaders. This training might involve theological education, lifestyle modeling, and meeting whatever other specific needs exist. *Unfortunately, this takes years of effort so other projects may need to be delayed until this can be accomplished. If a project needs to bypass local Christian leaders, it is a danger sign.* (Greer and Smith 2009, 255, emphasis added)

Unfortunately, the solution is beyond the scope of his organization and book. But the implications of his observations for a church-based approach to R&D are very important. If apostolic networks of churches are really to be at the core of a strategy for R&D, then there must be trusted leaders (elders, deacons, leading women, and others) in place to administer aid and money. And it is the work of apostolic leaders—that is, Ephesians 4:11 leaders—to train and establish other trustworthy leaders (Acts 20:17–38, 1 Timothy 3:1–16).

As will be noted in the last section of this chapter, Bryant Myers has written the most comprehensive survey and proposal for evangelical R&D in the literature. He has made the point that the evangelical academy has not done the sociological research needed to advance the evangelical voice and position in development work. Further, he addresses a theological gap:

> We are not even all that significantly involved in the religion and development conversation that has changed so dramatically in the last ten years.
>
> There has been little fresh thinking on *development ecclesiology*. Yet the question of the relationship between the Christian relief and development agency and local churches remains both unclear and problematic. (Myers 2011, 49, emphasis added)

Like Greer, Myers knows that working in and through local churches is challenging. Like several other authors, he does not back off of his endorsement of the local church as God's plan:

> At the end of the day, the work of holistic mission belongs to the church, not the development agency or the development professional per se. Tim Chester, formerly of Tear Fund UK, points out that "the New Testament does not describe development projects or, for that matter, evangelistic initiatives. Its focus is on Christian communities, which are to be distinctive, caring, and inclusive. Integral (holistic) mission is about the church being the church." . . .
>
> We need a new development ecclesiology that helps us understand local churches as both the gatherers and caretakers of local Christians and also as the expression of God's holistic mission.

> "One of the greatest challenges we Christians have at the threshold of the third millennium is *the articulation and practical implementation of an ecclesiology that views the local church, and particularly the church of the poor, as the primary agent of holistic mission.*" (Myers 2011, 191–192, emphasis added)

He's talking about Kingdom Outposts! Yet, like many of our evangelical authors, Myers's primary focus continues to be on the Christian development professionals and organizations that somehow need to partner with this entity called local church. He encourages development professionals to themselves be in a church and to see their work as a close partnership. He himself does not offer a "development ecclesiology," which would be beyond the scope of his own work. And his excellent work on transformational development continues to treat the church and development as two very different animals:

> The challenge is to find ways of using the Bible in human and social transformation that places the responsibility for asking questions of and seeking answers from the Bible within the community itself. I hasten to add that I am not saying that expository preachers or theological teachers are using inappropriate methods. In fact, exposition and formal teaching methods are ideal for church and classroom settings. I am saying that community development is very different and thus makes different requirements of us when it comes to using the Bible. (Myers 2011, 332)

It seems to be out of the question that a theological method involving a community hermeneutic *within the local church* could be a powerful source of doing Local Theology that leads to poverty reduction and human development. After all, church and community development are "very different."

Jayakumar Christian's *God of the Empty-Handed* is the finest attempt at a "development ecclesiology" reviewed in this thesis. Written by an Indian educated in the West, and with decades of poverty alleviation experience in India with World Vision, Christian is a biblical theologian and practitioner. His theological framework is a kingdom one, and particularly a kingdoms-in-conflict framework. He understands poverty as an issue of power at its core—one of powerlessness, god-complexes, and captivity. Christian believes the basic economic unit is not the individual but the household—the biblical perspective (1 Timothy 3:4; 5:8). He sees the local church not as a partner but as the agent of R&D:

> How do we equip the poor to become agents of transformation instead of being mere recipients of transformation? Underlying our commitment to do so is the belief that missional involvement among the poor must equip the church to trigger movements with the poor as the key agents of transformation. (Christian 1999, 10)

Christian particularly wants to attack the on-the-ground dichotomy that too many of the poor hold—the notion that the church is about spiritual things, but that you must look elsewhere for practical help:

During my data collection, the community was organizing to access bank loans to purchase livestock. Because of the project's success in tapping external resources, the poor in the community do not come to the church for any economic assistance; they go to the church to worship. Jayseelan, a local Christian politician, told me, "The church will take care of my relationship with God; in relation to the world and for doing good to my people, I need to work through the political parties." (Christian 1999, 128)

The church too often is "not part of the community's survival network... Could neglect of the social needs of the poor be a reason the poor neglect the church?" (Christian 1999, 104). Yet the biblical vision by necessity includes the church, that is, community. Evangelical theology across the board affirms that humans are made in the image of God, and this is a distinctive and crucial part of a sound R&D theology:

However, this belief that we are made in the image of God does not imply that we are finished products; we are *being made* in the image of God. This shaping of humans into the image of God is accomplished in the context of the church (that is, community). Therefore, community is an essential corollary to belief that we are made in the image of God. (Christian 1999, 128)

And this kingdom community does not simply respond to the poor out of humanitarian concern. Nor does it respond simply with human emotion or scientific technique. In fact, we are not the "first responder." God is.

> Kingdom power follows God's initiative. God hears the cry of the oppressed (Exodus 3:7,8) before calling for our involvement. God makes the first move. We are invited to work along with God in this awesome task of building the kingdom with a redemptive bias toward the poor. The Spirit's kingdom power affirms that involvement among the poor is an active response rather than simply a reaction. Neither compelling statistics about poverty nor our empowerment strategies will be the motivation in kingdom-based response to the poor. (Christian 1999, 204)

Christian also offers this critique of both sides of the secular or marketplace debate between bottom-up indigenous strategies and modern, Western top-down plans:

> It is no longer "power to the people" when kingdom power is exercised. Most participatory development strategies communicate the message that power belongs to the poor. Modernization strategies suggest that power belongs to the development and technical experts. Sometimes it seems that the church has bought into this philosophy of power rather naively. It is imperative that the church among the poor always communicate that the kingdom and the power do not belong to us... Power is a gift of God. (Christian 1999, 205)

A phrase that Christian uses, "covenant-quality community," parallels the phrase I've used, Kingdom Outposts:

> A kingdom-based paradigm will deal with relational dimensions [of poverty] by building covenant-quality communities that are inclusive. It will challenge the dividing lines. It will make the lines that divide a religious issue in which the God of history is interested... Kingdom-based response calls for building a covenant-quality community that points to the coming kingdom of God... If the powerlessness of the poor is the result of their captivity within many god-complexes in poverty situations, then these god-complexes must be confronted and dismantled... kingdom mission among the poor must involve prayer and fasting as important tools for social action... if kingdom-based response to the powerless involves confronting principalities and powers, then we should affirm that spiritual gifts are development skills required for responding to the powerless poor... equipping the church among the poor with the spiritual disciplines necessary for dealing with the rule of the Evil One. (Christian 1999, 213–218)

Within a covenant-quality community, Christian envisions members of that community as "grassroots practitioners." The members of this community need a new "alternative paradigm" of "re-equipping." He summarizes the program for establishing such a community in eight points (my words, not his):

1. The local church must establish full appropriation of a gospel identity, out of which flows our response to poverty.
2. The community (local church) is a demonstration project that models inclusive, truth-based relationships.
3. This community must be Spirit-led in order to confront principalities and powers, and plan for "intentional spiritual formation."
4. Leadership must equip members in their spiritual gifts for mission.
5. This community is a hermeneutical community acquiring skill in reading the Bible, which reveals the patterns of God's work among the poor.
6. Leaders need to equip the community to read the culture as well as read the Bible, being able to analyze the worldview of a people.
7. Truth and righteousness must become the hallmarks and battle cry of the community's own relationships, as establishing these in all relationships of the broader society is the kingdom mission.
8. Leaders need to equip the community to address global issues from a cosmic perspective, not just address local issues. As Christian writes, "Kingdom power seeks to cause ripples of transformation. Kingdom-based response equips the poor to be agents of transformation and thus initiates movements" (220–221).

Ultimately, Christian suggests that we completely rethink our categories of mission, mercy and justice, and R&D. We need to reframe our understanding of power, which is what kingdoms are all about. If we will do this, then poverty eradication ultimately is addressed when God's kingdom comes and his will is done, on earth as it is in heaven.

## Summary of Literature Review

Here in 2014, R&D and how to do it are hot topics, both in the marketplace and among evangelicals. While many on-the-ground initiatives continue doing business as usual, there is a clear consensus in the literature that we must do R&D differently. It will not do to keep mimicking past efforts—whether short-term Christian mission trips or extremely large USAID projects. R&D, as it has been practiced, has had too many wide-ranging unintended consequences to go along with its positive accomplishments.

The Global South is saying, "Listen to us!" No matter how well intentioned, and whether top-down or bottom-up, initiatives rooted in a "West knows best for the rest" are a problem. They often ignore the contributions and perspectives of local people. Further, they require expensive bureaucracies to administer the large programs and/or fundraising efforts. The South is telling us there's a better way. The way forward is some combination of international aid for large needs like roads and national medical care, along with local initiatives for business and job creation and simply getting needed cash to the "bottom billion."

Confronting cultural values and religious convictions is inevitable. Although culture change is off-limits in some of the secular literature, there is a growing awareness that it is part and parcel of eradicating extreme poverty. The literature is divided on whether religion is a problem or part of the solution. But a church-based theology, as articulated in chapter two of this thesis, clearly shows that biblical religion should be at the core of the solution. Christians have an enormous opportunity to contribute to the conversation and to demonstrate the power of Christ-centered culture change in bringing a reduction in poverty.

The church, particularly local churches, remains problematic. The secular literature either ignores the church or is afraid of its influence. The evangelical literature is extremely weak in offering a well-developed biblical basis for a development ecclesiology. The best of the evangelical literature points in the same direction as our biblical theology of the last chapter: we must undertake the long-term work of fully establishing local churches and local church leaders and their networks in the gospel of the kingdom, in the vision of the church as a Kingdom Outpost, and in a kingdom-framed vision of creation and economics. Unless this work is undertaken, we will continue to reproduce the ineffective mistakes of the past.

At the end of chapter two, we asked five evaluative questions of any approach, strategy, or theology of R&D:

1. Are local churches conceived of as the very locus of R&D? Or are they merely understood as sources of money and manpower?

2. Are local churches conceived of as Kingdom Outposts—in other words, is their life together characterized by kingdom values, economics,

and relationships? Is R&D accomplished by multiplying these outposts?

3. Are local churches understood to be part of broader apostolic networks? Are these church-to-church relationships characterized by kingdom fairness and the sharing of resources among each other?

4. Is R&D understood as part of salvation, a salvation that is carried to nations and civilizations by the planting and establishing of new Kingdom Outposts?

5. Is the underlying economic mind-set one of kingdom stewardship or pagan ownership? Is the attitude toward the earth, its creatures, and its gifts one of Western desacralized industrialism, or is it one of agrarian care for the sacred in the image of the land's Owner?

Almost all the literature, secular and evangelical, is rooted in secular ownership assumptions about markets, capital, property, profits, and money. As several authors pointed out, we evangelicals have naively held secular assumptions, some of which are profoundly opposed to God's values and his stewardship teaching. It is a desacralized view of land and economics when what is needed is an agrarian perspective as defined in this thesis. Only three of the authors make room in their approaches for the local church—Greer, Myers, and especially Christian. These three authors do make some progress on seeing the local church as the locus of R&D and acknowledging the necessity of a new kingdom economics within a local church. However, none of the literature addresses the strategy of the way of Christ and his apostles in establishing networks of churches linked together by apostolic leadership. No one sees church planting as the primary R&D strategy the church should be funding and promoting. And this author could find no real theological work in the R&D literature on salvation understood—in part—as economic provision now in this before-afterlife. In fact, as Berger pointed out in the quote above, in some ways the secular literature presents a more straightforward salvation than does the Christian literature, albeit in a desacralized gospel.

It appears that the perspective and approach offered in this thesis represent the outline of a genuinely fresh development ecclesiology, which may make a significant contribution to the conversation, as there appears to be almost no other voice offering a church-based, kingdom-framed understanding of relief and development.

CHAPTER FOUR:

# THE HAITICURE DEMONSTRATION PROJECT

HaitiCure is the name Lake Valley Community Church has given to our demonstration project in Haiti. The setting of this project was described in chapter one. Before narrating the project, several realities need to be addressed. As will be seen, HaitiCure is a mixture of success and failure. As a pilot project, it has been and continues to be a qualified success. A "proof of concept" project is just that; it reveals the strengths and weaknesses of the underlying concepts, and provides a laboratory for implementation efforts. In this regard, HaitiCure contains some failures. The failures in implementation will be noted as the project is narrated.

More significant, however, was the inadequacy of my own theology and knowledge of the relief and development literature when Lake Valley began HaitiCure. The theology outlined in chapter two, along with the survey and critique of the literature in chapter three, has been developed in parallel with the creation of HaitiCure. We did not understand four years ago what we now understand about Kingdom Outposts. We understand now that Kingdom Outposts are kingdom communities, established in the economic teaching of Christ and his apostles, living out their distinctive kingdom ethic and economics—and that these Kingdom Outposts are the locus and plan for R&D.

Also, Haiti is a particularly difficult setting, arguably the most difficult field for R&D in the western hemisphere. Only now, three years into the project, are we at Lake Valley gaining some measure of understanding of the particular challenges of Haiti. That, combined with our own growth in understanding this church-based paradigm, means we still have much to learn in years to come. That said, we now turn to narrating the project, with an analysis at the end of the chapter.

## HaitiCure Narration

In an email to Dr. Tim Boal dated October 19, 2010, I outlined a beginning strategy for Lake Valley's Integrated Ministries (IM) demonstration project in Haiti:

> Go2's IM Mission is to rebuild Haiti from within, through the church of Jesus Christ. Strategy is to (1) identify promising young Haitian leaders, (2) train and develop their character and capacity as kingdom leaders, and (3) resource them for success in building a civil society in Haiti.

Further, we set the following goals for the start-up effort in 2011:

- 2011 is a year for observing and listening. We need to refrain from overpromising, but rather assess and observe. We need to listen to Haitians' assessment of both their assets and their needs.
- We need to meet Haitians who are potential church and business partners.

- We need to solve some of the logistical problems of getting teams in and out safely and comfortably.
- We will take a trip to Haiti and focus on meeting leaders of church networks in Haiti, brokered by New York-based Haitian leaders.
- We would like to take a pilot group of Lake Valley members to Haiti in the summer to focus on the still-to-be-determined relief effort.
- We would like to coordinate a summer visit by some marketplace leaders to assess market-place projects.
- A visit in late summer or early fall will help nail down church partnerships for a five-year church establishment project in partnership with BILD.
- We will raise the $50,000 to $100,000 in seed capital to fund salary and travel expenses required to initiate the effort in Haiti.

In December 2010, we had agreed to sponsor a World Vision "Hope Sunday" for child sponsorships in Haiti. World Vision supplied folders for children from the Hinche area on the central plateau of Haiti. The children represented several of their Area Development Programs (ADPs). We hoped this would in fact contribute to the community development and personal education of these children, and we hoped it would focus Lake Valley's attention on Haiti and the need there. The New York City Leadership Center (NYCLC) thought that 50 to 75 sponsorships for a church our size would be successful. Lake Valley sponsored 128 Haitian children that December.

This was exciting to us, not least because of the economic potential. World Vision pays a "finder's fee" for facilitating child sponsorships. They know that it costs them around $200 to obtain a single sponsorship. So they are happy to enter into third-party agreements with organizations like the NYCLC that have demonstrated the ability to facilitate sponsorships. That single Hope Sunday at Lake Valley represented at least a $10,000 finder's fee. We began to think about promoting further World Vision sponsorships for Haitian children as a way into our church networks. If we could successfully invite other churches to implement Hope Sundays, perhaps this would be our "foot in the door" for further Go2 Integrated Ministries involvement in Haiti on the part of those churches. A "subcontractor" agreement with NYCLC could provide a $75 per sponsorship fee to Go2, which might become a helpful income stream for the organization.

## 2011: The First Year

The first nine months of 2011 were full of travel as we were moving up the learning curve. My past knowledge of child sponsorship agencies, NGOs, business-as-missions, microfinance, and facilitating large theological training projects was minimal. One of our elders, Roger Stanage, has facilitated many short-term mission trips in the past, had lived in Guatemala for two years, and had conducted successful construction projects in the developing world. He and I were in Haiti three times during the first half of 2011—again, primarily learning, observing, and meeting potential partners. In May, Jim Smith (a Lake Valley leader) and I went to the Dominican Republic next door to Haiti to see World

Vision's "ground game" there, visiting several of their ADPs and gaining a great orientation to their philosophy and organization. In July, I traveled to Tanzania with Compassion International in order to understand their approach to child sponsorship, which differs substantially from World Vision's.

World Vision is organized internationally as a partnership, with each country office having a large amount of autonomy. World Vision U.S. is focused primarily on fundraising for the rest of the partnership. In terms of World Vision's approach to development, their focus is not on individuals as much as it is on a child's whole community. So while child sponsorship with World Vision does indeed contribute to the personal education and health of the sponsored child, the bulk of the sponsorship money actually goes to health and infrastructure development in the child's community. These projects, known as Area Development Programs (ADPs), usually run ten to fifteen years, until the development work is done and programs are turned over to local leadership. Each ADP, which is run by World Vision staff, also includes recruitment and training of local church leaders in development work and in church cooperation for development work in that ADP. World Vision applies for matching grants from other governments and NGOs and is usually able to turn every dollar of child sponsorship donation into $1.50 to $2.

Compassion International is headquartered in the United States and is organized according to a more traditional business model, with more control centered in the home office. Compassion does not seek matching grants, believing this restricts their ability to evangelize and be explicitly Christian. They are more focused on the individual child being sponsored, with the bulk of the donor's money going directly to the health and education of the sponsored child and his or her immediate family. The model according to which Compassion delivers its services is, in its words, "church based." In any given city or area, one local church is selected by Compassion. A committee is formed in that church with extensive checks and balances in place for handling money. Money flowing into that area from Compassion donors is managed through that church's committee, with oversight provided by area Compassion staff.

Primarily because of our association with the NYCLC and our successful Hope Sunday event in December of 2010, we initially decided to partner with World Vision for the purposes of sponsoring children in Haiti.

Around that same time, I was also in Ames, Iowa, meeting with Jeff Reed of BILD and with Pastor Mullery Jean-Pierre from Brooklyn to discuss joining Mullery's team to deliver pastoral training in Haiti, using BILD's training materials and eventually enrolling Haitian leaders in their accredited Antioch School. Pastor Mullery's church, Beraca Baptist, had for years taken an annual summer short-term trip to Haiti. After the 2010 earthquake, they realized they needed to get more deeply involved in the development of Haiti and began making frequent trips to Port-au-Prince and Léogâne. Just west of Port-au-Prince, Léogâne, was the epicenter of the earthquake. Ninety percent of the buildings in Léogâne were damaged or destroyed. Beraca Baptist has sister churches in the area associated with their denomination and were in the process of implementing Rick Warren's

PEACE Plan in Léogane when we met. The PEACE plan is a holistic effort to *plant* churches, *equip* leaders, *assist* the poor, *care* for the sick, and *educate* (i.e., PEACE). They had a growing network of thirty to fifty pastors in Léogâne engaged in the PEACE Plan training.

Protestant churches experienced a boom in attendance and membership after the earthquake. Estimates I've heard range from a 50 to 100 percent increase in attendance, with anecdotes of many conversions and new members. Some estimate that the once Catholic and voodoo population of Haiti is now as much as 30 to 40 percent Protestant. We also learned that post-earthquake, many of the Protestant pastors and churches had come together for cooperation. We met several "leagues of pastors" during our trips.

One of these leagues, the Federation of the Leagues of Pastors of the Grand'Anse region, was headquartered in Jérémie, an eight-hour drive west of Léogane, out on Haiti's southern peninsula. They had invited Pastor Mullery to visit them, having heard some of his PEACE Plan sermons. Our Lake Valley team, consisting of myself and four leaders (Morgan Golden, Brady Helton, Donnie Wrublesky, and Roger Stanage), accompanied Pastor Mullery on the trip, meeting with the leadership committee of the league. The leadership committee is composed of eighteen men, representing several evangelical denominations with about 1,600 churches. They expressed a deep desire for theological training and help with economic development for their people.

Beraca Baptist Church had organized the Beraca Church Development Corporation (BCDC) for their new work in Haiti. Their vision was to combine evangelism, church planting, medical clinic work, and pastor training into one initiative. For instance, BCDC had obtained grant money from their denomination, Converge. One of the projects funded through this grant money is a motorcycle taxi business in Léogâne. Beraca is giving basic business training to Léogâne-area church members, and providing motorcycles to individuals who qualify. These new motorcycle taxi drivers pay for their motorcycles out of their business income, enabling Beraca to fund more drivers. They've put over fifty people in business so far. They also purchased land for a new church plant birthed out of their post-earthquake relief efforts, with room for a worship facility, BCDC offices, and housing for short-term ministry teams. As of 2014, this project is still under construction.

Beraca represented a great opportunity to us. BCDC is a church-based effort much like our fledgling work here at Lake Valley. It is a Haitian-led effort from the Haitian diaspora, focused on holistic development of their home country. Like us, they are learning the ropes of this kind of integrated work, and they have limited capacity. Beraca and its leadership were just beginning their own work in the Antioch School, while we had over ten years experience with a church-based approach to theological education here locally. We were eager to work with BCDC under Pastor Mullery's team leadership, to help him deliver leadership training for kingdom leaders in Haiti. By the fall of 2011, we had agreed to a partnership together for pastoral training, focused on Jérémie and Léogâne. Pastor Mullery would lead the team; my team and I would serve as support and provide much of the actual training at first, since we had been working with the BILD resources and the Antioch School courses for more than a decade. Over time, the actual training would be done increasingly by Pastor Mullery's team from Brooklyn and a team of Haitian leaders in-country.

While researching NGOs that might be involved in business development in Haiti, Roger Stanage came across an organization called Partners Worldwide (PW). I gave them a cold call early in 2011, speaking with Dave Genzink. It turned out he would be in Haiti at the same time as one of our scouting trips, so we made arrangements to meet there. When we did so, Dave was accompanied by Daniel Jean-Louis, head of their work in Haiti. Daniel was educated in the United States but has returned to live and work in Haiti in an effort to help his own country develop.

Partners Worldwide, an organization that has been around for almost two decades, is active in about twenty countries around the world. The organization specializes in finding existing small businesses in a country—small being one to ten employees—and partnering them with US business mentors. Partners Worldwide conducts basic business training for the national businesses and some basic cross-cultural missions training for the US mentors. The organization and the US mentors help in-country businesses create viable business plans, find reasonably priced sources of capital, and obtain loans when needed. The whole purpose is job creation. Doug Seebeck is the founder of PW, and his book *My Business, My Mission* was reviewed in the previous chapter.

During our meeting in Haiti, Daniel and Dave were discussing a new initiative they were preparing for their work in Haiti: the 100,000 Jobs Initiative. In a country of ten million people, there are only currently about 100,000 "on the radar" tax-paying jobs. PW would like to see that number doubled. They were ramping up a pilot project in the Léogâne area, with a goal of finding one hundred businesses in Léogâne to partner with US mentors. A group from Florida had committed to the first group of ten businesses, and as our conversation developed, they asked us to mentor the second group of ten.

We presented the opportunity to our Lake Valley businesspeople, and over twenty expressed an interest. We were especially glad to see that many of these were members who had been "on the sidelines." They were excited to have an opportunity to do ministry using the business knowledge and skills they had learned over the years. An initial group of a half dozen people went through PW's online training, and we began making plans to travel to Haiti to meet the ten businesses PW had vetted for us.

During the same trip on which we met the Jérémie League of Pastors, we also met our ten PW-selected businesses. They ranged from a small one-man bakery to a purified water business that employs around a dozen people. There was a community-based poultry cooperative as well as a small plantain farmer, and a young beekeeper with dreams of franchising his honey business so he could move up the production chain and become a honey wholesaler. We learned a lot as we helped PW finalize their assessment of these businesses, and a couple of businesses were eliminated. One business turned out to really be a front for procuring government and NGO grants. Nothing illegal was going on, but neither was there much—or any—actual production. The plantain farmer's business was so small and had such limited land that there was no potential for job creation.

Probably the most instructive case was the community poultry cooperative. It gave us firsthand exposure to the unintended consequences of well-meaning projects. We met one afternoon with an earnest group of community leaders in a hard-hit area of Léogâne. They had been trying to raise chickens for several months and were having trouble. An NGO had come to their neighborhood after the earthquake and built a large chicken coop for the community. We actually met in this facility; it was quite large. It was built of concrete and was certainly earthquake proof—very expensive. The NGO had provided feeders that used commercial feed, along with an initial flock of 250 chickens. The cooperative had been operating at a loss, and had begun slaughtering their brood of chickens for food. By the time we arrived, they were down to around fifty chickens. As we sat and talked, we did an informal unit cost analysis with them, and found quickly that they would never be profitable feeding chickens expensive imported commercial feed and trying to compete in the local Haitian market. We reluctantly advised them to abandon their current business and find another model for the community. As we talked, all around the NGO-built chicken coop were dozens of skinny-but-healthy free-range chickens (organic, no less!) foraging for free seeds and insects. This project was also eliminated from the program.

We committed to mentor six of the ten businesses, and PW began working on finding another four businesses for us.

By this time, we had also realized that our relationship with the NYCLC, while fruitful, was not going to deliver on-the-ground business development in Haiti. While the NYCLC was excellent in terms of convening and networking, they were not equipped or staffed to do the "blocking and tackling" of business development required to actually make progress in Haiti. So while we continued our partnership with the NYCLC, helping sponsor and design the second Movement Day in September 2011, we shifted our business development focus to Partners Worldwide.

In the fall of 2011, we believed we had learned enough to put together our first attempt to coordinate these three areas of partnership—World Vision child sponsorship, job creation with PW, and BCDC's holistic training with churches and pastors—and see if we could persuade other US churches to join us in Haiti. By now we were sure that short-term fixes were no fix at all in Haiti, given the long-term nature of the problems of poverty, governance, a poor business climate, and unestablished churches. We believed we would need to pilot a long-term approach. In light of some of the biblical work we had been doing, we were convinced that two institutions in Haiti desperately needed strengthening— the household, and the household of God. We still thought that our earlier observation about resourcing and training young leaders was important. It had also become obvious that young leaders need a context for training and development. Or to put it differently, so much of a leader's development is in the informal but nonetheless crucial formation of a family, and in the family of families—that is, the church.

At the September 2011 Movement Day Rebuild Haiti track in New York City, we made a short presentation of our project. We reported the following, reproduced from a handout:

Proof of Concept Phase. Léogâne, Haiti, and Lake Valley Community Church, Hot Springs, Arkansas

1. 128 Haitian children sponsored by Lake Valley Church through WV
2. 6 Léogane businesses being mentored, 25 Lake Valley business people mobilized
3. 50+ pastors and kingdom leaders in training in Léogâne area, in partnership with Rev. Mullery Jean-Pierre and the Beraca Community Development Corporation
4. This winter and into 2012 we will attempt to involve at least 12 additional churches in Hot Springs to sponsor 1,000 Haitian children, start several more Partners Worldwide affiliates, and involve at least four other Hot Springs pastors in leadership training.

We branded the effort HaitiCure and established a website, www.HaitiCure.com. We organized the effort into three categories: children, parents, and pastors. For the "children" category, we offered the opportunity to sponsor Haitian children through World Vision. The "parents" category represented our job creation initiative with Partners Worldwide. We hoped these two initiatives would prove viable ways to help strengthen households in Haiti. The "pastor" part of the initiative would be in partnership with Pastor Mullery and Beraca's BCDC initiative, along with BILD and their Antioch School. It was intended to strengthen churches by providing church-based theological training for pastors.

World Vision already had in place a robust sponsorship mechanism. Partners Worldwide had a brand-new sponsorship initiative called Dignity Partners. The Antioch School had been thinking about a sponsorship model, so for our project they put in place their first monthly sponsorship program: Antioch School sponsorships. Our effort would be two pronged—we would recruit local churches by approaching pastors in our area to do Hope Sundays and feature all three sponsorship options, and we would seek online sponsorships through social media marketing, which would direct donors to the HaitiCure website.

We rolled out HaitiCure in November and December of 2011. We spent several thousand dollars on local newspaper advertising, radio advertising, and targeted Facebook advertising to invite potential donors to the website, where all three sponsorship links were available. We mailed 150 area pastors an invitation to join us in sponsoring a Hope Sunday in December. I personally contacted nearly fifty of those pastors. Pastor John McCallum of First Baptist Church Hot Springs was enthusiastic about the project, and together we filmed a promotional video called "Hot Springs Hope for Haiti," which we posted on YouTube (http://youtu.be/ KPcF2Lk0wpo); we sent links to the 150 area churches.

We knew that the traditional way of recruiting churches into this kind of initiative is by conducting trips to the country, letting pastors and other leaders see the need firsthand. We were hoping that our local credibility and the awareness of Haiti as a result of the earthquake would allow us to bypass the traditional approach and do something more cost effective to open churches to our approach.

This initiative did not meet our expectations. After three months of promotion and about $4,000 in expenses, exactly one church had joined us in sponsoring a Hope Sunday—First Baptist Church. Our online marketing generated a lot of "click throughs" to our HaitiCure website, and exactly one actual sponsorship.

On the bright side, Lake Valley held its second Hope Sunday, and First Baptist held one as well. Between the two churches, another eighty children were sponsored with World Vision, along with six Dignity Partner sponsorships for PW and eight Antioch School scholarships.

# 2012: The Second Year

We went into 2012 debriefing the results of the church recruitment attempt and increasing our focus on Lake Valley's demonstration project in Haiti. After gaining some understanding in 2011, this was a year to do something.

## Children

The "children" category of the HaitiCure initiative was somewhat dormant in 2012. Lake Valley members

KINGDOM OUTPOSTS: A FRESH THEOLOGY OF RELIEF AND DEVELOPMENT

were continuing their World Vision sponsorships. We had a few meetings during the year to discuss coordinating a trip for church members to visit our sponsored children. World Vision's requirements for sponsor visits are strict, and it takes months to prepare for such a trip. Because of the demands on World Vision staff, they don't always say yes to a proposed visit. We also discussed getting our sponsors together for a "thank-you" celebration and to build further momentum. However, it's not possible to get donor information directly from World Vision, so we could only make a general invitation to World Vision sponsors; and we had hoped to include the broader Hot Springs community in the invitation. Lake Valley's leadership for the "children" category did not come together as we had hoped; hence this part of the HaitiCure initiative stalled, and nothing substantial was accomplished in 2012.

As 2012 came to an end, it was clear to us that if we were going to recruit other churches to join us, we were going to have to resort to the slower "vision trip" approach. As I write this, plans and funding are coming together for vision trips in 2014 to recruit—we hope—another dozen churches to sponsor children in Haiti through World Vision, and to sponsor parents and pastors through our other partners.

## Parents

Our parents initiative—job creation for families through partnership with Partners Worldwide—got off to a great start in 2012. For the first time, leaders other than Roger Stanage and me took trips to Haiti to visit our partner businesses in the Léogâne area. Paying their own way, two men (Bruce Dodson and Brady Helton) visited our businesses in January, and then one of our business couples (Larry and Holly Nieman) flew to Haiti in May. We were able to visit our businesses again in August, and a business couple from Ruston, Louisiana (Brian and Sarah Warren), conducted a one-day marketing seminar for our businesses, plus others who joined us. All of our businesses completed PW's basic business training in 2012. Several of them, along with their mentors, identified capital expenditure needs and put together successful loan applications for generators, concrete block vibration machines, conversion of a laundry's wood-fired boiler to propane, and other needs.

We did experience some growing-pain problems with the parents initiative in 2012. We were trying to visit our businesses more often than PW's standard of once a year, in order to help accelerate their 100,000 Jobs pilot program in the Léogâne area. However, travel and logistics in Haiti are still difficult and surprisingly expensive for such an impoverished country. The frequency of our business mentoring trips is under review right now. The Partners Worldwide staff in Haiti have also been strained by the growth of the Léogâne pilot, along with projects in several other parts of the country. Like all ministries, they can't afford to provide all the help that is needed. Our communication with our businesses flows through PW staff, primarily because of language barriers. None of us speak Creole. One or two of us have minimal French, which is not adequate for business discussions. Our mentors were finding communication slow and difficult.

Last, we have been increasingly interested in seeing the Christian business owners in Haiti become more established in their faith. While PW's training is biblically grounded and has a robust Christian ethic built in, it is not geared toward robust discipleship. The church, as a local entity, is entirely absent from their on-the-ground strategy. I was in Grand Rapids, Michigan, in 2012 to discuss with Doug Seebeck, Dave Genzink, and other PW staff the possibility of combining business training with theological training that is oriented toward potential kingdom marketplace leaders. As a result of these conversations, in October 2013 we began piloting a program in Jérémie that combines PW's business training and our theological training. Haitian PW staff member Oscar Antoine is our partner in this pilot project.

### Pastors

The pastor training initiative launched in January 2012. It quickly exceeded our expectations. My training team joined Pastor Mullery's team in Port-au-Prince for a pilot training session for leaders of the League of Pastors from the Léogâne area and from the Jérémie league. The proposal we made to the leagues was to use BILD's nonformal Leadership Mastery program to train pastors broadly. Then we would select the regional and national leaders who would benefit from an accredited degree through BILD's Antioch School. The Leadership Mastery program offers three levels of certification for a pastor or leader: Leadership Mastery 1, 2, and 3. Leadership Mastery Level 3 training is directly transferable into an Antioch School accredited bachelor's or master's program.

THE HAITICURE DEMONSTRATION PROJECT

The curriculum for the Leadership Mastery series consists of BILD's First Principles booklets, written by Jeff Reed. These booklets take a disciple through the didache, the apostle's daily life teaching from the New Testament epistles. Four booklets comprise Level 1, another nine booklets complete Level 2, and six of BILD's larger Leadership Series courses make up Level 3 training. Two representatives from Léogâne and two from Jérémie joined us in January to experience a training session for themselves and to make a final decision about bringing the training into their leagues. My team was joined for the first time by Gilles Marcouiller, a French-Canadian church planter and missiologist from Quebec, Canada. This pilot training was well received, with both leagues wanting to know when they could start.

As we debriefed from this experience, we had several observations. A consensus was developing that the top-level pastors could conduct discussions in French, but that most pastors would benefit greatly if Creole were used. BILD already had the First Principles booklets in French, but we also began thinking that a new Creole translation would be required in order for the training to be widespread, especially if it were to go beyond pastors to lay leaders and disciples. Pastor Mullery and his team also observed that the Léogâne area league was not as well organized as the Jérémie-based league. The decision was made for the Beraca church team to continue their PEACE plan training in the Léogâne area and use it to help the league recruit more pastors and prepare for the theological training. Pastor Mullery asked my team to take the lead in delivering theological training to Jérémie, as the material was fairly new to his team.

Thus, the following developed for pastor training in 2012:

- Both teams would travel to Jérémie in May to launch the training there.
- We would also use BILD's portfolio assessment tools to inject serious evaluation into the training.
- We would keep extensive records of pastors actually involved in the training for later documentation of the project.
- We would need about three days to take the pastors successfully through a BILD First Principles booklet.
- We would directly train the eighteen members of the league's council and challenge them to each train ten other pastors as part of their certification.
- We would attempt to form an Antioch School cohort as soon as possible and get some of these pastors enrolled in accredited degree programs.

The goal was a successful three-year training project in Jérémie that would serve as a model for other areas of Haiti, with the Léogâne area following close behind. During this three-year period, the Beraca Community Development Corporation would also be looking for regional and national leaders who could form a national team to take serious, ordered, church-based theological training across Haiti.

The May training was successful. The original eighteen members grew to about twenty-five league leaders, and they successfully completed the first booklet of their training. They were given ten booklets each, along with a portfolio assessment booklet. They were to reproduce with other pastors both the training and the assessment they had personally experienced. Today, they average eight pastors each, so altogether we have 225 pastors in training. In addition, the 200 in the "second wave" want to achieve BILD certification as well, so they are beginning to train other pastors and leaders. We are on track to have around 1,500 leaders in training in 2014 comprising the "third wave." We are currently working on a Creole translation of First Principles to facilitate this third wave of training.

In August 2012 our two churches—Lake Valley and Beraca Baptist—partnered together for a short-term mission trip. Mindful of some of the literature reviewed in this thesis-project, we tried to design a trip that would contribute developmentally to the Léogâne area. With Beraca Baptist Church and their BCDC in the lead, Lake Valley recruited about twenty men and women, ages sixteen to sixty, with a strong medical contingent. Our team was led by Lamar Trieschmann, pastor at Lake Valley, and Roger Stanage. BCDC had arranged for medical day clinics to be conducted in area churches, including their own church plant, accompanied by evangelism and children's ministries. The marketing couple mentioned earlier conducted a seminar for area businesses, and we were able to visit our Partners Worldwide businesses while in the area. About a thousand people were treated, but perhaps more important was the boost given to BCDC's holistic program as both businesses and churches were encouraged and strengthened. While still not the perfect model of a short-term trip, we felt that our partnership with a Haitian diaspora church and an in-country

KINGDOM OUTPOSTS: A FRESH THEOLOGY OF RELIEF AND DEVELOPMENT

Haitian-led network of churches—with them setting the agenda, not us—was a step in the right direction.

Immediately following the team's return to the United States, we flew to Jérémie for our second training, this time with just my team. We had extended this August training to four days in order to start an Antioch School Leadership Series course with five of the league's core leaders. This training was successful for the twenty-five league leaders, with them reporting that they were growing familiar with the method of delivery—a Socratic discussion approach—and that they had made their first attempt at evaluating their own trainees and filling out the portfolio assessment forms. We were able to complete about half of the Antioch School Leadership Series course with the five core leaders.

We were back in Jérémie in October 2012. This time Pastor Mullery's team was able to join us for part of the trip. We completed the third First Principles book with the twenty-five league leaders and completed the Leadership Series course with the five core leaders. We were also hit by hurricane Sandy during this trip; as a result, Pastor Mullery's team was delayed leaving Haiti, only to arrive in Brooklyn in time for the same storm to hit them again. Several people were killed in Haiti. The only road in to Jérémie was blocked by two mudslides, and the United Nations closed the only bridge into Jérémie, as the flooding river had washed out the bridge's foundations. My team's flight from Jérémie to Port-au-Prince was aborted twice due to winds and equipment failure. Finally, we flew out eight hours late. All in all, an eventful trip.

As we sat in the rain in Jérémie, we took time to generate a calendar and fundraising plan to complete the Jérémie project by the end of 2014. Our calendar has since been extended to March 2015 to complete the project. We returned in June of 2013 to complete Leadership Mastery Level 1 for the twenty-five league leaders. They received their certificates during our August 2013 training. Problems remaining to be solved include coordinating with the pastors' schedules. They all have other jobs, many as teachers. Currently, we are rearranging our training dates to accommodate their work schedules. The Creole translation of First Principles is in process, with the first booklet in Creole completed, and it's increasingly clear that it will be crucial to the effort. The five core leaders who completed the Antioch School course have not yet delivered their final project for review, and we are anxious to review and assess their ability to work at a seminary level.

So from a flat-footed start in January 2011, here's where the HaitiCure demonstration project stood two years later in the middle of 2013:

- About 200 children were sponsored through World Vision.
- The attempt to recruit churches using a local marketing campaign resulted in only one success.
- Six Haitian businesses were trained and mentored and now have access to affordable capital for expansion and job creation. Another fifteen businesses were recruited in the Jérémie area for the pilot of the combined business and theological training.

- Over 225 Haitian pastors received theological training, and we are on track to have at least 1,500 in training in 2014.
- Lake Valley Community Church experienced one-mindedness about Haiti—as over 120 families sponsored children, lay business leaders mobilized for the parent job creation initiative, and an apostolic team for the pastor training emerged within the congregation.
- We acquired eight full Antioch School scholarships to award to Haitian kingdom leaders; we are identifying an emerging national team and forming a cohort.
- We entered into a young but promising partnership with a Haitian diaspora church, Beraca Baptist of Brooklyn, New York, and their BCDC holistic initiative in Haiti.
- Over $100,000 was released for mission work— over and above Lake Valley's normal operating and mission (Establishing) budget—with no negative impact on our overall giving. In fact, 2012 was the biggest giving year on record for Lake Valley, even as we struggled to recover from the Great Recession of 2008. Approximately $1,060,000 was given to the normal operating budget. Another $60,000 annually was being released through child sponsorships and will be ongoing for some years to come. The funding for HaitiCure appears to be new money that would not otherwise have turned up in our offerings.

# Analysis

As noted at the beginning of the chapter, the HaitiCure project was undertaken before I had completed the theological work of this thesis—and before I had accomplished a complete interaction with the current R&D literature. HaitiCure has been the impetus for the research, and the research in turn has informed the project. At the end of chapter two, five questions were proposed to evaluate R&D arising out of a biblical theology of God, his people, and his land. These five questions were then used to critique the R&D literature reviewed in chapter three. The HaitiCure project will now be analyzed using these same questions.

## 1. Are local churches conceived of as the very locus of R&D? Or are they merely understood as sources of money and manpower?

The HaitiCure project did not conceive of our own local church, nor of the churches in Haiti, as the locus of R&D. At the time we had a fairly conventional view of evangelical R&D, with two important advances. One, we wanted our efforts to be church-based. Two, we wanted to avoid the kind of mistakes introduced to us by books like *When Helping Hurts*. Because of our mind-set several years ago, we thought that Lake Valley would be doing all the R&D work—in other words, church-based from here in the United States—and that Haitian households and churches would be recipients of these smarter efforts as outlined in *When Helping Hurts*. That is how the project was structured, and that is how the money flowed, around the categories of children, parents, and pastors.

Better still would have been an understanding that envisioned well-established Haitian Kingdom Outposts providing R&D for their own country. In and through these outposts, the needs of children and their parents would be met. In and through these outposts and their networks, the training of apostolic and local church leaders would be accomplished. This would have altered many of our approaches. For instance, different partners or partnership arrangements would have been necessary. Our partnership with BCDC would have been the primary partnership, rather than being one of three equal partners. Further, Beraca Baptist itself and its BCDC initiative require further theological development and understanding of this Kingdom Outpost paradigm. As Greer points out (and as noted in chapter three), the training of reliable local church leadership should take priority over other R&D projects (Greer and Smith 2009, 255). A mutual learning process with Lake Valley and Beraca Baptist of Brooklyn would have been an ideal scenario, with the goal of training and mobilizing cohorts of apostolic and local church leaders in Haiti to in turn establish Kingdom Outposts, which in turn would function as the locus of R&D for their local communities in Haiti.

This certainly does not rule out the possibility or desirability of partnering with organizations like World Vision or Partners Worldwide. It does mean, however, that these partnerships need to be arranged so they serve the ultimate end of a movement of Kingdom Outposts being established. This would require more dialogue and work to ensure that partners are aligned with a Kingdom Outpost vision for R&D.

World Vision is a problematic partner. They represent a non-church-based approach to relief and development. They are a huge organization and the bureaucracy is difficult to work through. The reputation of World Vision Haiti is spotty, receiving mixed reviews from the Haitians we've consulted. On the other hand, they have an extensive ground operation in place. We were impressed with their operations in the Dominican Republic next door to Haiti. They do reach out to churches in their Area Development Programs, offering training in community development and fostering cooperation among local churches for development. There may well be a tremendous opportunity to partner with World Vision Haiti and add church-based theological training to their existing local church work.

Partners Worldwide is perhaps the best of the BAM organizations we've found thus far. They have a proven training model, and their core concept of partnership is a great advance over more colonial "the West knows best for the rest" strategies. They have a strong systematic, Reformed theological base. Our partnership with them has been fruitful, and it is characterized by a great sense of piloting together the best approach for job creation in Haiti. Their lack of involvement with the local church in Haiti is unfortunate, while understandable in light of some of the difficulties working with local churches, as detailed in chapter three. We are hoping to bridge that gap with them and see business and theological training combined for marketplace Kingdom Outpost leaders.

Beraca Baptist Church and the Beraca Community Development Corporation represent a great opportunity in Haiti. With Pastor Mullery Jean-Pierre's leadership, there is the potential of a truly Haitian multiplication movement to establish Kingdom Outposts in Haiti. They too are learning this new paradigm. Many of their efforts thus far have been rooted in the typical evangelical R&D paradigm critiqued in this thesis. But their instincts have been toward a more holistic kingdom approach for the *shalom* of their home country.

If we are to produce the "development ecclesiology" that Bryant Myers calls for in *Walking with the Poor*, then the first step is to understand the *ecclesia*—the local church—as the locus of R&D.

## 2. Are local churches conceived of as Kingdom Outposts—in other words, is their life together characterized by kingdom values, economics, and relationships? Is R&D accomplished by multiplying these outposts?

We had almost no understanding of kingdom economics when HaitiCure was launched. We certainly were aware of the apostles' teaching in the New Testament on caring for widows and orphans, the dangers of wealth, the importance of giving proper respect and care to the poor, and all the rest of the apostolic teaching mentioned in chapter two. However, we had no understanding of that teaching as growing out of the major biblical theme of the land and its use for the R&D of the people of God and, by extension, the people of the earth. Our training of Haitian parents (namely, those who were business owners) and pastors was devoid of the theological economic framework outlined in this thesis.

We knew that involvement in HaitiCure would cost Lake Valley money, and we understood that as part of our kingdom perspective and desire to be used in the spread of the kingdom. We hoped that this R&D project would further disciple Lake Valley economically into a kingdom heart and mind. We were not as clear on our hopes for Haitian churches. We were primarily focused on the needs of existing pastors for further theological training. We did not yet have a clear vision for what their churches might become or what kind of churches might be planted as a result of that training.

We had a relatively good understanding of the broad outlines of a Kingdom Outpost. The apostles laid out the major components of a fully established Kingdom Outpost in their epistles. These are the major truths that were to be understood and lived: (1) the gospel of the kingdom; (2) the church and its structure and leadership; (3) the church's kingdom mission; (4) the Holy Spirit, who advances the kingdom; and (5) a kingdom and mission hermeneutic of the Bible. A summary of these as a brief overall definition of "Kingdom Outpost" can be found in the appendix. Not included in that summary in the Appendix is the more particular economic vision of this thesis of the gospel of the kingdom, the economic life of the church, and the economic component of the church's mission, which is R&D. That will be summarized below.

KINGDOM OUTPOSTS: A FRESH THEOLOGY OF RELIEF AND DEVELOPMENT

### 3. Are local churches understood to be part of broader apostolic networks? Are these church-to-church relationships characterized by kingdom fairness and the sharing of resources among each other?

We were on the front end of understanding what a modern-day apostle is and what apostolic networks might look like when we started HaitiCure. The Lake Valley elders understood this enough to allocate half of my time to this project while continuing my full financial support. As we entered a partnership with Mullery Jean-Pierre, we learned the importance of an indigenous Haitian apostolic leader being on point for the pastor component of HaitiCure. An apostolic team has also emerged inside Lake Valley through the course of this project. There are now a half dozen leaders who function directly as modern-day Pauls and Timothys—and as coworkers like Epaphroditus or Aquila and Priscilla, not to mention as financial benefactors for the project.

We've also grown in our understanding of the relationships between apostolic leaders. We now see that HaitiCure is being carried out by a network of apostolic teams: my team that has emerged at Lake Valley and our network of churches based on informal relationships; Tim Boal's team under the banner of the Go2 Network, rooted in the Grace Brethren network of churches but not limited to that; Jeff Reed's apostolic team, which is how BILD and the Antioch School function, along with their network of churches using their models and resources around the world; and Mullery Jean-Pierre's team headquartered in Brooklyn, along with his denominational network among the Haitian diaspora in the

United States. At this point, which team is "in the lead" depends on the particular task being accomplished. For instance, when it comes to the implementation of Haitian pastor training, all the teams defer to Mullery Jean-Pierre's team, as it is his network and his country in which we are working.

So while the structure and implementation of HaitiCure did not always reflect this understanding, one of the major long-term successes of the project has been the achievement of some understanding of both the theory and practice of apostolic leadership and networks.

Further, it has become clear that a focus on apostolic leadership is more strategic than just a generic focus on leadership development or pastor training. The training of Ephesians 4:11 apostolic leaders is a highly leveraged, strategic approach that makes the best use of limited manpower and money. Our initial instinct, mentioned in chapter one, was to train young kingdom leaders, whether they are clergy or marketplace leaders. This instinct proved correct. We go even further now, sharpening the focus to say that the most strategic way to advance the mission of establishing Kingdom Outposts that are the locus of R&D is to identify, equip, and release apostolic leaders.

### 4. Is R&D understood as part of salvation, a salvation that is carried to nations and civilizations by the planting and establishing of new Kingdom Outposts?

It is now. We entered into HaitiCure believing that (1) the kingdom is spread through the establishing of churches and (2) salvation is entry into the kingdom now and in the life to come. This is why the project was designed to be church-based. In this sense, HaitiCure was well designed and implemented. However, it must be said that my personal understanding of R&D in 2010 was that it is a grateful response to salvation. In other words, as the love of God through Christ saves and forgives us, one of our grateful responses is love of neighbor—namely, R&D work. This is true to some degree. However, I have now come to the understanding that R&D is not a *response* to salvation; rather it is a *component* of salvation. God cares about our economic imprisonment and wants to rescue us from it. Our experience of his provision and care in the before-afterlife continues into the afterlife and is consummated in the after-afterlife. The framework of this understanding was presented in chapter two. Jayakumar Christians *God of the Empty-Handed*, reviewed in chapter three, is a fine resource for this perspective.

### 5. Is the underlying economic mind-set one of kingdom stewardship or pagan ownership? Is the attitude toward the earth, its creatures, and its gifts one of western desacralized industrialism, or is it one of agrarian care for the sacred in the image of the land's owner?

This was not consciously part of the design of the HaitiCure project. However, one of the first things we learned about Haiti, from Haitians, was their desperate ecological crisis. The deforestation of the country has had devastating economic effects. In order to have a small cash income, the poor burn the trees into charcoal, which can be sold for use in cooking stoves. They also sell the wood for laundries (a major small-business sector in Haiti). We were excited when one of the partner businesses we are mentoring wanted to convert their laundry boiler from wood to propane. Not only did it make economic sense for the business; it was a demonstration of how to relieve the pressure on the few remaining forests of Haiti.

The pastors and churches we have met thus far in Haiti seem to have no concept of the relationship between Christianity and ecology. Church takes care of spiritual afterlife matters; deforestation is a secular issue. If the churches and Christians of Haiti could learn the Bible's agrarian perspective and how it applies to our contemporary world, they could be a force for the good on behalf of the land and people of Haiti.

This is also true of Lake Valley Community Church. Since the start of HaitiCure, I have had occasion to preach on this theme as I have learned it myself, and it has been received with a mixture of appreciation, irritation, and opposition. Could it be that the answer to some of our ecological crises in the world is the establishment of Kingdom Outposts in those cultures and places that will then demonstrate and advocate for the care of God's land?

## Marks of a Kingdom Outpost

So what are the marks of a Kingdom Outpost being fully established in a kingdom economics? The following eight marks of a Kingdom Outpost are based on the teaching of chapter two and the analysis of chapter three:

1. *Sacredness*. The biblical truth is taught and believed that the earth, its resources, and its

inhabitants are sacred because they exist by the will and breath of God: "In him we live and move and have our being" (Acts 17:28). The underlying paradigm of the Kingdom Outpost is that we are tending a sacred garden while we work toward and hope for the heavenly city. An agrarian perspective as described in chapter one is taught. Kingdom Outposts practice and advocate for creation care, in order to feed and care for humanity.

2. *Blessing*. Kingdom Outposts recognize that the earth is given for the blessing of all humanity, and that the people of God are called to be the locus of that blessing for all humanity. That means a Kingdom Outpost is characterized by an outward mind-set—namely, it exists not solely for the sake of its members but for the sake of others. "Election" is understood as a missional category; we are chosen to bless others as we participate in the spread of the kingdom. Projects, actions, and initiatives intended to bless others economically are ongoing in and through the outpost (see *The Hole in Our Gospel*, chapter 18, "Putting the American Dream to Death").

3. *Sharing*. Sharing is taught among the people of God. Modeled on the wilderness and land ethics taught in the Torah, the sharing of money and resources is practiced—not only for the benefit of Christians but also for the "aliens" among us who come into our communities of faith and need help. Personal profits and portfolio growth are sacrificed in order to share with others. There

will be mechanisms, programs, and initiatives within a Kingdom Outpost to appropriately share money and opportunity with the poor (microfinance and credit unions, for instance, as described in *The Poor Will Be Glad*).

4. *Stewardship.* Those who have wealth and power— that is, the "kings" among the people of God— are taught that they are stewards, not owners. Their wealth exists for the advantage, mission, and good of the whole faith community, not just for their own. They are discipled in an ethic of justice and righteousness and are expected to use their power on behalf of the people of God and the "aliens" among them. They are accountable to God and to the community for their stewardship. Greed is taught to be a sin. Wealthy disciples are not only freely and generously giving to the poor; they are discipling others into stewardship.

5. *Accountability.* The entire Kingdom Outpost understands that it is accountable to God for its economic life together and its treatment of the poor—Christian and non-Christian—among them. This means that prayer and fasting are often focused on the outpost's use of its funds and influence, discerning God's will for their use (see *Fast Living*). Offerings and church budgets are judged not just on their size but on their use and apportionment. The percent of the outpost's budget dedicated to the poor will be large, and it will increase as the Spirit directs.

6. *Love.* Jesus' summation of the Torah will be the measure for evaluating the outpost's use of

its wealth and treatment of the poor: Are we using our wealth to increase our love of God and neighbor? Are we being good neighbors, going out of our way to sacrificially help those in need—even across racial, cultural, and geographic boundaries? Do we have an arrogant "god-complex" (see *When Helping Hurts*) or a heart full of grateful love and mercy toward the poor? A Kingdom Outpost understands that poverty is ultimately a kingdom issue of power, and it depends on the cross of Christ and his resurrection power to defeat the power of death and poverty (see *God of the Empty-Handed*).

7. *Fairness.* The apostolic teaching regarding wealth and the economics is a major part of the discipleship ministry of the Kingdom Outpost. The elders and leaders of the outpost shepherd the flock so that the poor are honored and have enough money and provision; the rich are not becoming arrogant and selfish and thus hurting themselves; and needs are wisely matched up with resources so there is a fairness both perceived and practiced in the body of Christ. The local outpost also sacrifices wealth and sends money to help other outposts in need, through trusted apostolic networks for dispersal by trustworthy local leaders. Money actually flows around, in, and through the outpost so that apostolic leaders are released, local leaders in other places are developed, economic needs are met, and envy and greed are reduced.

8. *Mission.* The Kingdom Outpost understands that its mission is not only concerned with afterlife salvation. It also looks forward to an after-afterlife consummation and realizes that all of its R&D work now in the before-afterlife is valuable and will not be wasted in light of the resurrection (1 Corinthians 15:58). A Kingdom Outpost teaches that there is a before-afterlife component to salvation (and lives in light of this reality). In other words, economic provision and fairness are intended by God for all humanity and are part of his mission and his salvation plan for mankind. Understanding that this economic component of salvation comes to people as the kingdom of God comes to them, the Kingdom Outpost devotes people, leaders, money, prayer, and partnership for the planting and establishing of even more Kingdom Outposts, both locally and globally, as its primary plan for R&D.

# CHAPTER FIVE

# KINGDOM OUTPOSTS AND RELIEF AND DEVELOPMENT

Relief and Development is not in the Bible—at least, R&D as usually conceptualized by US evangelicals. Instead, the Bible contains a vision for a new humanity alive on this earth, hoping and working for the renovation and re-creation of a new earth. This new humanity is living in a new (old) way. As detailed in the summary at the end of chapter two and in the description of Kingdom Outposts at the end of chapter four, a Kingdom Outpost's life together is characterized by economic fairness, which involves the following components: a kingdom economics rather than a capitalist or a socialist economics; the absence of either greed or laziness; the absence of poverty; trustworthy, well-established leadership that can dispense money and care wisely; a welcoming attitude toward outsiders; and care for anyone in the outpost's sphere of influence. Kingdom Outposts are much more than "church" as we usually conceive of it here in the United States. They are not sources of R&D. They *are* R&D.

Their vision, their assumptions, the obstacles they see, and the means they use are radically different from both the marketplace version of R&D and the existing evangelical version.

# Vision

R&D as usually practiced is a vision of a better future for humanity. It is a future that will be better because more and more people will have the opportunity to help themselves, to better themselves financially, to be educated, to be healthier. This future is usually painted in terms of health, wealth, education, "quality of life," economic opportunity, and access to capital and markets. It is a future where hard work is rewarded and the playing field is fair and level. While not all will enjoy the same results, all will have the same chances. Families can build cities, which in turn can build nations, which can build civilizations. Autonomous freedom is the goal: freedom to decide how high you want to climb, freedom to pursue those dreams, freedom to compete fairly, freedom to try and fail and try again. Wealth and autonomous freedom and power have been the vision since time began—consider Babel, Egypt, Assyria, Babylon, Greece, Rome, and now America.

God's Kingdom Outposts have a different vision, one of a redeemed future for humanity. The goal is not simply a "better future" but a re-created future—a future where not only is our economic poverty fixed but the poverty of our rebellious relationship with our Creator is forgiven and healed, the poverty of our greedy use of his creation is healed, the poverty of our broken relationships with one another is reconciled, and the poverty of our inner shame and bankruptcy is cured.

It is a comprehensive vision of salvation, both now and in the age to come. God's kingdom is not merely looking for the advancement of the human condition; it is looking for an advent—a second advent where the promise of his Kingdom Outposts is fully realized in the whole earth. A future with not only more money in our pockets but a new Spirit in us. A future where the goal is not autonomous freedom but the freedom to love and serve God, one another, and God's creation.

These different visions are undergirded by differing assumptions as well.

## Assumptions

R&D assumes that wealth is an unmitigated good and that more money, more buying power, and more access to capital are essential ingredients of the good life. Conventional wisdom is that there is no downside to money—quite literally, "the more the merrier." The success of R&D efforts is measured by the increase of jobs, income, gross national product, and money spent on health care and education. The love of money is assumed to be a good thing, as long as enough opportunity is present and markets are free. Enlightened self-interest will keep everything in balance. Ownership, the ability to own land and control your own capital, is the hallmark of a successful development program and the formation of a robust, sustainable economy.

The kingdom of God assumes that wealth (mammon) is a spiritual force and a dangerous tool that easily turns into an idol of destruction. Scripture teaches that more contentment and more godliness are better than more money. Christ and his apostles warn that there is a huge downside to money. It traps those who want to be rich. It competes quite effectively with the worship of our Creator, demanding its own worshipful sacrifices. It prevents people from entering into God's kingdom, especially when their own kingdom is going so well— as Jesus says, "How difficult it is for those who have wealth to enter the kingdom of God!" (Luke 18:24). Wealth is meant to be used as a tool for true worship and salvation; it is not meant to be melted into a golden calf for our own pleasure or benefit. The love of money does indeed make the world go 'round as the love of money is the root of all kinds of evil—and this world is currently under the spell of evil. Furthermore, ownership is a prideful sin in the kingdom. "Stewardship" is the kingdom value. Everything belongs to the one true Owner, the God and Father of Jesus Christ. We live as tenants in the house he built. And we steward the wealth he entrusts to us. The success of kingdom expansion through the establishment of Kingdom Outposts is evidenced by the increase in *shalom*—less violence, more sharing and fairness, safety, enough to eat and drink— in the midst of "Babylon." There should be an increase in mercy and justice, love of God and neighbor, and the generous care of the poor and weak. Right relations with the creation, its creatures, and our fellow human beings will be on the increase.

## Obstacles

R&D sees all its obstacles. That is to say, we can see the realities that need to be dealt with. We can see the corruption, the closed markets, the faulty models, the unjust laws. What we can see, we can fix. We can develop our way to a desacralized salvation. But conventional R&D only sees the tip of the iceberg.

The kingdom model would not disagree with what is seen. What is seen is real. But it also sees the unseen real. There really is supernatural evil that hates humanity and loves cruelty and poverty. There really are principalities and powers, and it is these with which we wrestle. Money is not a-spiritual. Money and wealth have unseen but real spiritual forces behind them. A Messiah was needed in order to deal with the unseen real. A cross was required, as was a resurrection. That Messiah's Spirit had to wash over and indwell a people, changing them from the inside out. His Spirit changes their inner unseen real into a real, seen community.

## The Means

R&D proponents will work with almost anyone. But the more powerful the agent, the better (of course). Foundations, businesses, nonprofits, militaries, large donor bases, governments, corporations, and courts are all potential agents of R&D. Most conversations about R&D make only a passing reference to churches. Occasionally, someone will notice that churches represent an enormous potential resource. If only all these churches could be harnessed as partners and donors for R&D. They could be a great source of money and volunteer time needed for R&D activity.

The gospel of the kingdom does not see churches as partners in R&D. In the kingdom, churches *are* R&D.

Churches are the locus of kingdom R&D, not a provider of agents and agencies to do R&D outside the church. They are Kingdom Outposts. They are preaching and living salvation—eternal life *now* and in the life to come. Life together within the new communities of Jesus, when lived faithfully to the gospel, is a life of economic sharing, fair and equitable distribution, mercy and justice, care for the poor, encouragement of responsibility, discouragement of laziness, valuing contentment, promoting stewardship of the earth, and sharing of markets and capital and opportunity generously:

> It is in this light that we must understand the purpose and goal of missions... Sometimes the emphasis is on the conversion of the greatest possible number of individuals and their incorporation into the Church. The success of the mission is to be evaluated in terms of church growth. Sometimes the emphasis is on the humanization of society, the eradication of social ills, the provision of education, healing, and economic development. Success in either of these aims is hailed as success for the mission. By contrast St. Paul's criterion seem to be different... [When] he has, in his own words, "fully preached the gospel" and left behind communities of men and women *who believe the gospel and live by it...* [then] his work as a missionary is done. (Newbigin 1989, 121, emphasis added)

So the spread of the blessings of the kingdom to all humanity is not accomplished by spreading techniques of R&D but by spreading Kingdom Outposts. Planting and strengthening kingdom communities that live by our Creator's land ethic and image, walking in his ways, living by his Spirit. *Establishing Kingdom Outposts is the R&D plan of Christ and his apostles.*

## Further Reflections on the HaitiCure Demonstration Project

The HaitiCure project has been an interesting mix of learning, disappointments, and accomplishments. I have gained enough clarity about the establishment of Kingdom Outposts that I now see the early stages of the project as not fully thought out or developed. This of course is the nature of proof-of-concept initiatives and demonstration projects. In retrospect, when the project began in January 2011, we had two basic aims: (1) to be faithful to the Scriptures in light of what we had learned thus far about church-based theology and ministry, and (2) to eventually involve other US churches in Go2 Network's Integrated Ministries. As Lake Valley Community Church got deeper into the demonstration project, our energy shifted to some degree into making the project work. While the demonstration project is not yet finished, we are well into it now and are finally at a place to assess the project and identify next steps, both for Go2 Network and Lake Valley.

We are encouraged that a church of our size and location could find quality partners and manage an attempt at a church-based, Integrated Ministries approach to R&D. The following are main takeaways from the HaitiCure project thus far.

- Apostolic leadership is key. By *apostolic*, I mean leadership that is sent out, as Antioch sent Paul and Barnabas (see Acts 13:1–3), to establish churches. Apostles are the leaders Christ gives to the church for its establishment and equipping, as detailed in Ephesians 4:1–11. Other New Testament examples include Timothy and Silas, Peter, Epaphroditus from Philippi, and Paul's coworkers Aquila and Priscilla. Whether on an apostolic team or leading such a team, these individuals focus on the regional and global expansion of the kingdom through establishing churches. Whether on the US side or in Haiti, leaders who are fully committed to the local church but also have a global calling and gifting are indispensable. Leaders and pastors who are primarily called to local church shepherding and eldering are key players but will not generate the apostolic initiative required.

- Our projects need to be more focused geographically. If we were starting over today, we would wait until all three areas of work—children, parents and pastors—could be accomplished from one geographic hub in Haiti. Currently, we are scattered from the extreme southwestern tip of Haiti to the central highlands.

- Our partners need to be more closely aligned. This is a tall order, and to some degree beyond our control. Going forward, we will be seeking partners who understand or who are willing to learn the vision of Christ and his apostles for R&D work—that is, establishing Kingdom

Outposts. As a start-up initiative, we have faced the constant tension between us and our more experienced partners, who see in us leaders who can get the job done and want us to help with *their* vision and agenda.

- Go2's Integrated Ministry work will not generate a revenue stream that can fund further staff hiring beyond those doing actual IM work. There is some income available through commissions for sponsorships. Charging short-term teams a fee can cover a living expense for a staff person—who would then be consumed by recruiting and running those short-term trips.

- US church recruitment is difficult at best. Churches are already overwhelmed with appeals for money and child sponsorships. Many pastors are extremely careful about anything that might compete with the weekly offering. Missions budgets are already fully assigned. We believe we'll have to take a slower approach to US churches, perhaps focusing more on younger church planting movements that already possess a more missional outlook.

- We are happy to answer with a resounding yes to the root question—Can a local US church get beyond just sending checks to missionaries and parachurch organizations and generate an Integrated Ministries approach internationally?

- The concept of strengthening households and churches is the right concept. The focus on education and health of children and their communities, job creation for parents, and the strengthening of pastors holds good promise. While more integration of programming for children, parents, and pastors is needed under the umbrella of establishing Kingdom Outposts, the basic idea is sound.

- Lake Valley is a US church of modest size. Having concentrated our missions efforts, it has been very encouraging to see what we've achieved. Many other US churches could achieve similar results if their energy and dollars for missions were more focused.

- Multiplication approaches have tremendous potential. Our children and parents initiatives do not represent multiplication strategies. The pastors initiative, however, is considered a multiplication movement, thanks to the movement and multiplication orientation of the BILD resources and paradigm. Because of this, after just a few years, we have a large number of pastors receiving training.

## Potential Contribution of This Thesis-Project

I believe that the church-based theological framework outlined in this thesis could make a substantial contribution to the R&D conversation among Christians. The biblical theology of the land outlined earlier is a corrective to our afterlife-only notion of salvation and could completely reframe the R&D conversation in the literature. Moreover, I believe the main proposal of this project—that we should be pouring our R&D efforts and money into planting and strengthening Kingdom

Outposts and kingdom leaders—could bring immense focus and effectiveness to evangelical missions and development efforts.

The HaitiCure project is strengthening households and churches in Haiti. Networks of churches and individual churches associated with the League of Pastors in Jérémie will be strengthened and put on a path of learning the biblical theology outlined in this thesis. We are contributing to Beraca Baptist Church and their BCDC project as they learn this church-based paradigm as well. Lake Valley has mobilized itself in the direction of becoming a Kingdom Outpost itself, and we will have further influence in our network of churches.

Lake Valley is in the early stages of applying the lessons of this thesis-project to our region of the United States. In our training room at Lake Valley, we keep a map of Haiti on the wall to remind us of the HaitiCure project. We also keep a map of our region, consisting of the states of Arkansas, Louisiana, and Mississippi. These three states have about the same population as Haiti. Like Haiti, they have a strong French cultural influence. This part of the United States is one of the poorest regions in the country, particularly the Mississippi Delta area of all three states. We are just beginning to ask ourselves how we should think like missionaries in our region, in light of what we've learned through this thesis-project.

This thesis-project has already been an informal resource to other churches in our network and their own R&D efforts. It is hoped that the fruit of this work will more formally help shape their own projects and, more importantly, help shape these churches into Kingdom

Outposts. We hope the thesis can become a resource for the establishment of new churches in our network.

While this thesis has taken a biblical theology approach, perhaps it can make a contribution to those working in a systematic theology framework as well. As noted throughout, this understanding of Kingdom Outposts could contribute to soteriology, missiology, and ecclesiology. Further, some of the practical considerations gleaned from the literature and the HaitiCure project could make a contribution to practical theologies and resources developed for short-term teams and mission pastors.

Pastors, missions pastors, missions committees, missionaries, parachurch organizations, professors of missiology—anyone associated with Christian R&D efforts—ought to wrestle with the perspective offered in this thesis-project. Without a doubt, convincing many people of this perspective will be a long, uphill struggle. But there are many of us who feel unsettled, who know something is ineffective or even wrong with our current approach. Some of us who are restless about these things will have to be the paradigm pioneers who demonstrate a better way:

> Once again it has to be said that there can be no going back to the "Constantinian" era. It will only be by movements that begin with the local congregation in which the reality of the new creation is present, known, and experienced, and from which men and women will go into every sector of public life to claim it for Christ, to unmask the illusions which have remained hidden and to expose all areas of public life

to the illumination of the gospel. But that will only happen as and when local congregations renounce an introverted concern for their own life, and recognize that they exist for the sake of those who are not members, as sign, instrument, and foretaste of God's redeeming grace for the whole life of society. (Newbigin 1989, 232)

## Further Study and Next Steps

Further theological work needs to be done on the land motif in the New Testament. Land theology has been hijacked by competing eschatologies and dispensational hermeneutics. More work on the fulfillment and extension of land theology by Jesus and his apostles should yield a richer understanding of salvation and the mission of the church. I believe this biblical theology of land has the potential of correcting both replacement theologies and artificial dispensational schemes, and healing the false dichotomy of salvation versus social action.

Because of what I've learned about the land theology of the Bible, I believe there is great potential in an "agrarian theology" of church and church planting. The apostle Paul reminded the believers at Corinth that he "*planted*," Apollos "*watered*," and God gave the "*growth*"—in fact, they are "God's *field*" (1 Corinthians 3:5–9, emphasis added). I have several questions I would like to explore in the future. For example, are our American church models essentially industrial models? If so, how would an agrarian model be different? In addition to social action, should ecological interests also be part of our gospel? How would our concepts of pastors, elders, church staff, and missionaries be different in an agrarian model? What would it mean to reject abstract, industrial, top-down solutions to church planting in the United States and adopt an agrarian "local theology" strategy instead?

> Local adaptation, then, is authentically a scriptural issue and so an issue of religion. It is also the issue most catastrophically ignored in the economic colonization of American landscapes and in the industrialization of agriculture. Now in the presence of much destruction, we must ask the questions that this book makes obvious: Was not the original and originating catastrophe the reduction of religion to spirituality, and to various schemes designed exclusively to save the (disembodied) soul? Could we have destroyed so much of the material creation without first learning to see it as an economic "resource" devoid of religious significance? Could we have developed a reductionist science subserving economic violence without first developing a reductionist religion? What would America be now if we white people had managed to bring with us, not just a Holy Land spirituality, but also the elaborate land ethic, land reverence, and agrarian practice meant to safeguard the holiness of the land? (Wendell Berry, in the foreword to Davis 2009, xii)

Lake Valley needs to grow toward becoming a fully established Kingdom Outpost itself. In light of the eight marks of a Kingdom Outpost at the end of chapter four, Lake Valley needs to take the following steps:

- We need to teach in as many venues as possible the *sacredness* perspective of the Scriptures, as a response to the unbiblical industrial view of the earth and its resources. This agrarian perspective needs to become part of the culture of Lake Valley. Some resources will need to be created for this effort.
- Lake Valley does a good job of *blessing* Hot Springs. We need to extend our efforts to our region of Arkansas, Mississippi, and Louisiana, particularly the Delta region.
- We have had informal meetings and conversations about *sharing* at Lake Valley. It is time to establish Lake Valley funds, foundations, banks, credit unions, or whatever mechanisms are appropriate for sharing resources. A team or advisory board needs to oversee this effort, under the direction of the elders.
- We have given several sermons recently on *stewardship*, going so far as to state that an ownership attitude is a sin. We now need to recruit a few of our wealthy disciples and further ground them in this perspective and let them, in turn, disciple others in the church. This could be the beginning of a group of benefactors for Lake Valley—a recognized team of leaders in the fields of wealth and stewardship—who become instrumental in funding the ministry and mission of Lake Valley and its apostolic team.

- We need to teach the congregation the truth that there is *accountability* to God for our economic life together. Our elders need to analyze and adjust our budget and budgeting process in light of our theology of Kingdom Outposts, setting challenging targets for our R&D spending. We need to call the church to prayer and discern how much of our wealth should be devoted to the poor among us and to the poor in our surrounding community who may turn to us for help. The spiritual gifts of helping, serving, and giving should be taught and honored more.
- Lake Valley has recently summarized its strategy with the following four words: gathering, growing, serving, and sending. We need to particularly frame up serving as a *love* response, not simply a *duty* response. Knowing that the kingdom of God is in conflict with the kingdoms of this world, we need to equip the congregation with an Ephesians 6 understanding of kingdom conflict, in the larger context of serving one another and our community as a Kingdom Outpost.
- *Fairness* needs to be taught more explicitly from the pulpit, in our small groups, and in our discipleship groups. Our elders and deacons need to begin prioritizing programs and mechanisms within the life of Lake Valley, in order to increase both the perception and reality that fairness is being achieved in our life together. This should be one of their major ministries. An accessible way for the poor to request and receive help needs to be defined. Money needs to be given away under

wise leadership. As we establish trustworthy partners in our region and globally, we need to start sending cash gifts to impoverished congregations.

- We need to begin planning and resourcing for the *mission* of planting new Kingdom Outposts in Hot Springs, Garland County, Arkansas, Louisiana, and Mississippi. We have a young network of like-minded churches in our city and region that are interested in this endeavor. We need to resource and further release our resident apostolic team so they can identify, equip, and release other apostolic leaders in our region—both in the church sphere and the marketplace—who will start Kingdom Outposts. We will probably need to use a variety of strategies like traditional church planters, organic house churches, grassroots missional communities, and others we haven't seen yet.

The HaitiCure project will continue until our current commitments are fulfilled, which will probably run through March of 2015. The time frame depends primarily on the speed at which our Haitian partners are able to complete the Pastor's First Principles training. The next steps for the work in Haiti, which do not have to wait until the current work is finished, appear to be as follows:

- Entering into conversation with World Vision Haiti about cooperating with their efforts to train local church pastors, offering a church-based theological training system

- Continuing our efforts to sponsor a total of 1,000 Haitian children through our network.
- Running a pilot with Partners Worldwide in which a local Haitian church becomes deeply involved in vetting businesses for PW and in which kingdom-oriented theological training is offered alongside business training. This step also involves exploring the possibility of using the pastoral leagues in Haiti as paths for business development and for the identification of apostolic marketplace leaders.
- Sharpening the focus of BCDC's pastoral training. We could spend years doing general pastoral training in Haiti. Almost every pastor we've talked to in Haiti wants more training. However, we need to take what we've learned from the Jérémie and Léogane league training and begin focusing on equipping Haitian apostolic leaders. Some of these leaders will be clergy, perhaps others will not. Our bias needs to be toward younger men and women as well. We need to form a truly national team of Haitians—both diaspora and in-country—to lead a Kingdom Outpost movement across Haiti.
- Raising more money. We need $150,000 to finish the first phase of HaitiCure. To date, $50,000 of that amount has been raised. We would like to see a network of churches support this work, along with a few large donors and many small donors.
- Coaching a few other US churches in similar initiatives, whether in Haiti or elsewhere.

# A Theological Manifesto

Jesus taught that the kingdom of God has come and that he intends to set the captives free, proclaiming the good news to the poor that the year of the Lord's favor—Jubilee—has dawned. Jesus has bound the strong man so we can plunder his house. The apostle Paul reminded us that we wrestle against cosmic powers and spiritual forces of evil over this present darkness. We need to recover the biblical truth that this conflict of kingdoms is happening now, not in the distant past or in an afterlife future. And we need to recover the truth that human poverty is one of the ways evil oppresses and imprisons humanity. The kind of desperate, grinding poverty that enslaves billions of humans in our day is evil.

Conventional R&D efforts, whether secular or evangelical, often offer a desacralized vision of salvation from the evil of poverty. These efforts attempt to deliver the benefits of God's salvation without the scandalous cross of Christ. We are often proclaiming a message of hope in democracy and capitalism, instead of hope in the resurrection of the Lord Jesus and its power to transform us and our cultures. We evangelicals, who pride ourselves on our defense of biblical truth, have too often been seduced by this new gospel of R&D. And to be fair, the desacralized gospel of R&D has arisen, in part, because the churches of Jesus Christ have ignored or been ignorant of biblical teaching on God's people as the locus of R&D. Because we have framed salvation as only an afterlife issue of heaven or hell, we have been on the sidelines far too often as evil poverty has crushed the bodies and souls of men, women, and children around the world.

Salvation is also a before-afterlife issue. Some of us need to repent of our "lifeboat theology"—that is, the belief that the world is going to sink anyway, so our only task is to drag a few disembodied souls into the lifeboat as we sail away into the afterlife. God's vision is that the whole creation and all its creatures will be redeemed. This redemption *begins* now through the chosen people of God, and it will be consummated in the second advent of the Lord Jesus. Jesus came preaching the message of this kingdom of blessing and *shalom*, and he meant for the message and the reality of his kingdom to spread over the earth, to every tribe and nation.

The kingdom of Jesus spreads and takes root in cultures, nations, and civilizations through the establishment of Kingdom Outposts. These local communities of Jesus have a distinctive life together. We are used to the idea that their life as a church should have a distinctive sexual ethic, or a distinctive family ethic, or a distinctive honesty ethic. We are *not* used to the idea that these Kingdom Outposts should also have a distinctive economic ethic. In fact, they should have a distinctive economy—whether their surrounding culture is communist, socialist, or capitalist. These outposts are designed to be demonstration projects of a kingdom economy that is shaped by the creation ethic, wilderness ethic, and land ethic of God's people of Israel, now inherited, fulfilled, and extended to the whole earth through Jesus Christ and his apostles and the church.

Therefore the primary task for Christians, if we are going to do battle with the evil of poverty, is to put personnel, money, and energy behind the planting and strengthening of Kingdom Outposts, making sure that these outposts are well established in the apostolic teaching, and rooted in the Old Testament teaching, of kingdom economics. These Kingdom Outposts and their economic life are marked by the teaching and practice of *sacredness*, *blessing*, *sharing*, *stewardship*, *accountability*, *love*, *fairness*, and *mission*. The establishment of Kingdom Outposts, that have a financial life marked by these truths, is the way of Christ and his apostles for relief and development.

# APPENDIX

Early in 2012, I was challenged to condense my convictions about Kingdom Outposts and missions. The result is the following handout, put together for distribution in October 2012 at the Movement Day event in New York City:

## KINGDOM OUTPOSTS
### Dru Dodson

I have been in a learning community for some years now, studying the Scriptures almost every week together. It's been a very serious, ordered experience. And for the most part we've used guides published by BILD (www.bild.org). The process has been great for leadership development, and some of us are pursuing accredited degrees now (www.antiochschool.edu). One of the primary truths we have learned from our study concerns the biblical teaching of "establishing." The Greek New Testament word is 'steridzo,' often translated "strengthening." It's used in the New Testament in the context of "*establishing* the church" or "*strengthening* the believers."

It's a core concept because it begins to define the goal of all of our mission effort; church programs and efforts; relief and development efforts; training programs, etc. And once you clearly define the goal, you begin to see the implications for the "how tos" of doing your missions, programming, relief work. Paying attention to establishing is not a quick path to "best practices" that will numerically grow your church or ministry. It's not a "plug and play" program or curriculum. It's more like the binary code or operating system that works behind any number of apps. Getting ahold of the idea and implementing it has changed our lives and is bearing much fruit among us. What follows is a little summary of the concept and some of its implications.

"When is a church a church?" Missional communities, house churches, megachurches, organic churches, Bible studies, parachurches, mission agencies—when is a group of Christians classified as a church? Lots of ink spilled on this. A lot of money is at stake. Millions of dollars have been raised and spent on planting churches, resulting in thousands of groups of people in homes and huts, gathered around a Bible. Does that count? Was that good return on the millions of dollars? Five years later, how many of those groups still exist? How many are growing and thriving?

We've found there is a better question! It's much more helpful to ask, "When can a group of people, a community, be said to be an *established* church?" We actually have answers to that question in our Bible! This requires reading and studying the New Testament documents—Gospels and Epistles—*not* as systematic theology treatises or devotional stories, but instead reading them as church-establishing documents. They were all written from within Jesus communities, and they were written to other Jesus communities, in order to strengthen those new Kingdom Outposts. What are the marks of these strong communities—these fully established Kingdom Outposts?

*A Kingdom Outpost is a fully established community of disciples of Jesus.* We avoided using the word "church" in that sentence because of all the assumptions and cultural expectations that kick in when you say "church." A Kingdom Outpost is certainly a church, in the timeless New Testament sense. It may or may not look like our typical North American expectation of "church."

An *established* Kingdom Outpost is experiencing the gospel daily, is missional in orientation because of that gospel, functions as a family of families in the family order of Christ and his apostles, and not only lives by the Spirit but is keeping in step with the Spirit as he spreads the kingdom of God.

Jesus called his message "the gospel of the kingdom." His message produces Kingdom Outposts, not just kingdom individuals. These Kingdom Outposts can be said to be strong, or established, when we evidence the following marks as a community of disciples of Jesus:

1. THE GOSPEL OF THE KINGDOM—we have internalized and embraced it and guard it. The whole promise plan/metanarrative of God's redeeming work is intended to bless all the world, redeeming both creation and creatures, winning the conflict/war with evil. It is the promise and fulfillment of a King and his kingdom, the outpouring of his Spirit, the filling of the Spirit. Internalizing this gospel involves the integration of head and heart in receiving the gospel. It is experiencing the power of the gospel in the "inner man" and the healing and release from shame and guilt. When we embrace this gospel,

we begin to live an integrated life of shalom and blessing and are given a new identity and a new heart—finally becoming fully human!

2. THE MISSION OF THE KINGDOM—we have adopted it as our own. We receive this gospel for ourselves, but not just for ourselves. We are saved for the sake of others! We are chosen for others! We are chosen, elect, predestined—not to fly away to heaven but to spread the good news here. We are announcing and living out the defeat of sin and death, inviting others out of the kingdom of darkness into the kingdom of light. We are seeking the *shalom* of our fallen planet and its sinful civilizations, and we are looking forward to a new heaven and earth. We are making the gospel beautiful and believable. We understand that this movement spreads through the establishing of more Kingdom Outposts.

3. THE PEOPLE OF THE KINGDOM—we have oriented our lives to one another. We receive the gospel not just as individuals but as a community. The gospel is grafted into a movement, adopted into a new family. We orient our lives to the life and mission of the people of God. We understand the organic nature of the church as a people, a body, and a movement—and as God's plan A. We are being trained in the teaching about daily life relationships in the body. We are a peculiar people, an alternative society. Our life together is the best apologetic for our faith. We follow the apostles' teaching on leadership roles and responsibilities

in a church. This includes teaching on leading and following; eliminating the split between clergy and laity and between sacred and secular; church discipline; household order; sodality and modality structures in the kingdom community. We are Ephesians 4:11 equippers. Our outpost is an environment of grace with relationships of trust.

4. THE SPIRIT OF THE KINGDOM—the Spirit has filled us and leads us. Salvation is not solely about going to heaven someday; salvation is life in the Spirit now. Our life is summarized as "If we live by the Spirit, let us also keep in step with the Spirit" (Galatians 5:25). We are redoing our evangelical transactional/contract understanding of salvation into a relational life-in-the-Spirit concept. We are focusing on the following: manifestations and gifts of the Spirit; life change; miracles; fruit of the Spirit in our lives; Spirit power; understanding ourselves biblically as a "charismatic" movement. We believe "the kingdom of God does not consist in talk but in power" (1 Corinthians 4:20).

5. THE BOOK OF THE KINGDOM—we're learning how to read it! Our biblical theology involves gaining a Jesus hermeneutic, a love application grid, and a promise-plan metanarrative. We are learning that the message of the Old Testament is the same as the New and that the hermeneutical "key" is understanding Jesus'

kingdom teaching. We are gaining a church-based hermeneutic, a missional hermeneutic.

In other words, an established church is engaged in the reproducing cycle of engaging, equipping, and establishing other strong Kingdom Outposts. We believe that serious attention to this teaching of Christ and his apostles, and the way they went about establishing the movement, will save us from our addiction to American definitions of success-as-numbers, our consumer orientation in the church, our misunderstandings of what a pastor and other leaders are supposed to do, and our multiplication of shallow, weak—but often large—churches.

It's time we get "S.M.A.R.T." about church planting and start establishing Kingdom Outposts.

## The SMART Mission

SHALOM of the whole earth is the goal. Kingdom Outposts are societies of justice and mercy. We enjoy a right relationship with our Creator, with his creation, and with people made in his image. "Your kingdom come, your will be done, on earth as it is in heaven" (Matthew 6:10). Kingdom expansion extends beyond economic development, evangelism, or free-market capitalism.

MULTIPLICATION of established Kingdom Outposts is how *shalom* spreads over the earth. Relief and development or "justice and mercy projects" are not outside activities in which the community of Jesus participates by providing money and volunteers. The new communities of Jesus—Kingdom Outposts—are not the agents of *shalom*; they are the location of *shalom*! They are demonstration projects, proof-of-concept initiatives.

APOSTOLIC leaders and their teams lead the multiplication of Kingdom Outposts, shepherding and linking together the Kingdom Outposts. These leaders from all walks of life need to be identified, equipped, and released for kingdom expansion.

RELATIONSHIPS of trust and environments of grace form the apostolic leaders, the kingdom culture of the kingdom movement, and its Kingdom Outposts. New gospel identity and new gospel living lead to the transformation of individuals, families, clans, tribes, cities, societies, nations, and civilizations.

THEOLOGICAL training for kingdom leaders from all walks of life is needed, not just for clergy. The future is releasing mission-minded marketplace leaders who have a robust theology of the gospel of the kingdom, a kingdom theology of money and power, and are committed to the shalom of the world through multiplying Kingdom Outposts.

Dru Dodson
Lake Valley Community Church, Hot Springs, AR www.lakevalleychurch.com
Go2 Network, Telford, PA
www.go2ministries.com
drudodson@gmail.com
Twitter: @drudodson

# REFERENCES

Aristide, Jean Bertrand. *In the Parish of the Poor: Writings from Haiti*. New York: Orbis Books, 1990.

Banerjee, Abhijit V., and Esther Duflo. *Poor Economics: A Radical Rethinking of the Way to Fight Global Poverty*. New York: Public Affairs, 2011.

Berger, Peter L. *Pyramids of Sacrifice: Political Ethics and Social Change*. New York: Anchor Books, 1976.

Berry, Wendell. "The Agrarian Standard." *Citizenship Papers*, 143–152. Washington, D.C.: Shoemaker & Hoard, 2003.

———. "Economy and Pleasure." *What Are People For? Essays by Wendell Berry*, 129–144. Berkeley: Counterpoint Press, 2010.

———. *The Long-Legged House*. Washington, D.C.: Shoemaker & Hoard, 2004.

Bishop, Matthew, and Michael Green. *Philanthro-Capitalism: How the Rich Can Save the World*. New York: Bloomsbury Press. 2008.

Blocher, Henri. *In the Beginning: The Opening Chapters of Genesis*. Downers Grove, IL: InterVarsity Press, 1984.

Brown, William P. *The Ethos of the Cosmos: The Genesis of Moral Imagination in the Bible*. Grand Rapids, MI: Eerdmans, 1999.

Brueggemann, Walter. *The Land*. Philadelphia: Fortress Press, 1977

Burge, Gary M. *Jesus and the Land: The New Testament Challenge to "Holy Land" Theology.* Grand Rapids, MI: Baker Academic, 2010.

Chester, Tim, ed. *Justice, Mercy, and Humility: Integral Mission and the Poor.* Carlisle, UK: Paternoster Press, 2002.

Christian, Jayakumar. *God of the Empty-Handed: Poverty, Power, and the Kingdom of God.* Monrovia, CA: World Vision International, 1999.

Collier, Paul. *The Bottom Billion: Why the Poorest Countries Are Failing and What Can Be Done About It.* Oxford: Oxford University Press, 2007.

Corbett, Steve, and Brian Fikkert. *When Helping Hurts: How to Alleviate Poverty Without Hurting the Poor and Yourself.* Chicago: Moody Publishers, 2009.

Davis, Ellen. *Scripture, Culture, and Agriculture: An Agrarian Reading of the Bible.* Cambridge: Cambridge University Press, 2009.

Davis, Mike. *Late Victorian Holocausts: El Niño Famines and the Making of the Third World.* London: Verso, 2001.

De Waal, Alex. *Famine Crimes: Politics and the Disaster Relief Industry in Africa.* Bloomington, IN: Indiana University Press, 1997.

DeYoung, Kevin, and Greg Gilbert. *What Is the Mission of the Church? Making Sense of Social Justice, Shalom, and the Great Commission.* Wheaton, IL: Crossway, 2011.

Easterly, William. *The White Man's Burden: Why the West's Efforts to Aid the Rest Have Done So Much Ill and So Little Good.* New York: Penguin Books, 2006.

Eberly, Don E., ed. *The Essential Civil Society Reader: The Classic Essays.* New York: Rowman & Littlefield Publishers, 2000.

————. *The Rise of Global Civil Society: Building Communities and Nations from the Bottom Up.* New York: Encounter Books, 2008.

Eisenberg, Evan. *The Ecology of Eden.* New York: Knopf, 1998.

Eldred, Ken. *God is at Work: Transforming People and Nations Through Business.* Montrose, CO: Manna Ventures, 2009.

Ellerman, David. *Helping People Help Themselves: From the World Bank to an Alternative Philosophy of Development Assistance.* Ann Arbor, MI: University of Michigan Press, 2005.

Farmer, Paul. *AIDS and Accusation: Haiti and the Geography of Blame.* Berkeley: University of California Press, 1992.

———. *Haiti After the Earthquake.* New York: Public Affairs, 2011.

———. *The Uses of Haiti.* Monroe, MA: Common Courage Press, 2006.

Foshee, Andrew W. "The Political Economy of the Southern Agrarian Tradition." *Modern Age.* Spring 1983, 161–170.

Greer, Peter, and Phil Smith. *The Poor Will Be Glad: Joining the Revolution to Lift the World Out of Poverty.* Grand Rapids, MI: Zondervan, 2009.

Grigg, Viv. *Companion to the Poor.* Tring, UK: Lion Books, 1984.

Gutiérrez, Gustavo. *A Theology of Liberation: History, Politics and Salvation.* New York: Orbis Books, 1988.

Hallward, Peter. *Damming the Flood: Haiti, Aristide, and the Politics of Containment.* London: Verso, 2008.

Hanlon, Joseph, Armando Barrientos, and David Hulme. *Just Give Money to the Poor: The Development Revolution from the Global South.* West Hartford, CT: Kumarian Press, 2010.

Harrison, Lawrence E., and Samuel P. Huntington, eds. *Culture Matters: How Values Shape Human Progress.* New York: Basic Books, 2000.

Hauerwas, Stanley. *The Peaceable Kingdom: A Primer in Christian Ethics.* Notre Dame, IN: University of Notre Dame Press, 1991.

Hays, Richard B. *The Moral Vision of the New Testament: Community, Cross, New Creation: A Contemporary Introduction to New Testament Ethics.* New York: Harper-San Francisco, 1996.

Hiebert, Theodore. *The Yahwist's Landscape: Nature and Religion in Early Israel.* New York: Oxford University Press, 1996.

Huber, Richard. *The American Idea of Success.* New York: Pushcart Press, 1987.

Hunter, James Davison. *To Change the World: The Irony, Tragedy, and Possibility of Christianity in the Late Modern World.* New York: Oxford University Press, 2010.

James, Erica. *Democratic Insecurities: Violence, Trauma, and Intervention in Haiti.* Berkeley: University of California Press, 2010.

Johnson, C. Neal. *Business as Mission: A Comprehensive Guide to Theory and Practice.* Downers Grove, IL: InterVarsity Press, 2009.

Kaiser Jr., Walter C. Toward *Rediscovering the Old Testament.* Grand Rapids, MI: Academie Books, 1987.

Keller, Timothy. *Generous Justice.* New York: Dutton, 2010.

Kristoff, Madeline, and Liz Panarelli. "Haiti: A Republic of NGOs?" U.S. Institute for Peace, *PeaceBrief* 23 (April 26, 2010).

Lausanne Committee for World Evangelization. *Business as Mission.* Lausanne Occasional Paper No. 59. 2004 Forum for World Evangelization.

Lints, Richard. *The Fabric of Theology: A Prolegomenon to Evangelical Theology.* Grand Rapids, MI: Eerdmans, 1993.

Lupton, Robert D. *Toxic Charity: How Churches and Charities Hurt Those They Help (and How to Reverse It).* New York: HarperCollins, 2011.

Maguire, Robert. *Haiti Held Hostage: International Responses to the Quest for Nationhood, 1986–1996, Occasional Paper #23.* Providence, RI: Thomas J. Watson Jr. Institute for International Studies, Brown University, 1996.

Maren, Michael. *The Road to Hell: The Ravaging Effects of Foreign Aid and International Charity.* New York: The Free Press, 1997.

Metraux, Alfred. *Haitian Voodoo.* Trans. Hugo Charteris. New York: Schocken, 1972.

Moeller, Susan D. *Compassion Fatigue: How the Media Sell Disease, Famine, War and Death.* New York: Routledge, 1999.

Moyo, Dambisa. *Dead Aid: Why Aid Is Not Working and How There Is a Better Way for Africa.* New York: Farrar, Straus, and Giroux, 2009.

Myers, Bryant L. *Walking with the Poor: Principles and Practices of Transformational Development.* Maryknoll, NY: Orbis Books, 2011.

Narayan, Deepa. *Voices of the Poor: Can Anyone Hear Us?* New York: Oxford University Press for the World Bank, 2000.

Newbigin, Lesslie. *The Gospel in a Pluralist Society.* Grand Rapids, MI: Eerdmans, 1989.

———. *The Open Secret: An Introduction to the Theology of Mission.* Grand Rapids, MI: Eerdmans, 1995.

Nicholls, B., ed. *In Word and Deed: Evangelism and Social Responsibility.* Exeter, UK: Paternoster, 1985.

Pamphile, Leon Denius. *Haitians and African Americans: A Heritage of Tragedy and Hope.* Gainesville: University of Florida Press, 2003.

Petrella, Ivan. *The Future of Liberation Theology: An Argument and Manifesto.* Aldershot, UK: Ashgate, 2004.

Pogge, Thomas. *World Poverty and Human Rights.* Cambridge, UK: Polity Press, 2008.

Polman, Linda. *The Crisis Caravan: What's Wrong with Humanitarian Aid?* New York: Macmillan Books, 2010.

Prince, Rod. *Haiti: Family Business.* London: Latin American Bureaum, 1985.

Reed, Jeff. *The Churches of the First Century.* Ames, Iowa: The Biblical Institute of Leadership Development, 2009.

———. *The Paradigm Papers.* Ames, Iowa: The Biblical Institute of Leadership Development, 1992–1997.

Robinson, Randal. *An Unbroken Agony: Haiti, from Revolution to the Kidnapping of a President.* New York: Basic Civitas Books, 2007.

Rodin, R. Scott. *Stewards in the Kingdom: A Theology of Life in All Its Fullness.* Downers Grove, IL: InterVarsity Press, 2000.

Rundle, Steven, ed. *Economic Justice in a Flat World: Christian Perspectives on Globalization.* Colorado Springs, CO: Paternoster, 2009.

Rundle, Steven, and Tom Steffen. *Great Commission Companies: The Emerging Role of Business in Missions.* Downers Grove, IL: InterVarsity Press, 2003.

Russell, Mark L. *The Missional Entrepreneur: Principles and Practices for Business as Mission.* Birmingham, AL: New Hope Publishers, 2010.

Sachs, Jeffrey. *The End of Poverty: Economic Possibilities for Our Time.* New York: The Penguin Press, 2005.

Sailhamer, John H. *The Pentateuch as Narrative: A Biblical-Theological Commentary.* Grand Rapids, MI: Zondervan, 1992.

Schmemann, Alexander. *For the Life of the World: Sacraments and Orthodoxy.* New York: St. Vladimar's Seminary, 1988.

Schmidt, Hans. *The United States Occupation of Haiti, 1915–1934.* New Brunswick, NJ: Rutgers University Press, 1971.

Schwartz, Glenn J. *When Charity Destroys Dignity: Overcoming Unhealthy Dependency in the Christian Movement.* Lancaster, PA: World Mission Associates, 2011.

Schwartz, Timothy. *Travesty in Haiti: A True Account of Christian Missions, Orphanages, Food Aid, Fraud and Drug Trafficking.* Lexington, KY: Self-published, 2010.

Seebeck, Doug, and Timothy Stoner. *My Business, My Mission: Fighting Poverty Through Partnerships.* Grand Rapids, MI: Partners Worldwide, 2009.

Sen, Amartya. *Poverty and Famines: An Essay on Entitlement and Deprivation.* London: Oxford University Press, 1981.

Sider, Ronald J. *Rich Christians in an Age of Hunger: Moving from Affluence to Generosity.* Nashville: Thomas Nelson, 2005.

Smith, Stephen C. *Ending Global Poverty: A Guide to What Works*. New York: Palgrave Macmillan, 2005.

Stearns, Richard. *The Hole in Our Gospel*. Nashville: Thomas Nelson, 2009.

Todd, Scott C. *Fast Living: How the Church Will End Extreme Poverty*. Colorado Springs, CO: Compassion International, 2011.

Volf, Miroslav. *Work in the Spirit: Toward a Theology of Work*. Eugene, OR: Wipf & Stock Publishers, 2001.

Walton, John H. *Ancient Near Eastern Thought and the Old Testament: Introducing the Conceptual World of the Hebrew Bible*. Grand Rapids, MI: Baker Academic, 2006.

Williams, Eric. *From Columbus to Castro: The History of the Caribbean, 1492–1969*. London: Andre Deutsch, 1970.

Winter, Bruce. *Seek the Welfare of the City: Christians as Benefactors and Citizens*. Grand Rapids, MI: Eerdmans, 1994.

Wirzba, Norman. *The Paradise of God: Renewing Religion in an Ecological Age*. New York: Oxford University Press, 2003.

World Bank. *Doing Business 2010: Haiti*. Washington, D.C.: The International Bank for Reconstruction and Development, 2009.

———. "Doing Business in Haiti." *Doing Business 2013: Smarter Regulations for Small and Medium-Size Enterprises*. Washington, DC: World Bank Group, 2013.

Wright, Christopher J. H. *God's People in God's Land: Family, Land, and Property in the Old Testament*. Grand Rapids, MI: Eerdmans, 1990.

———. *The Mission of God: Unlocking the Bible's Grand Narrative*. Downers Grove, IL: InterVarsity Press, 2006.

———. *The Mission of God's People: A Biblical Theology of the Church's Mission*. Grand Rapids, MI: Zondervan, 2010.

Wright, N. T. *Surprised by Hope: Rethinking Heaven, the Resurrection, and the Mission of the Church*. New York: HarperCollins, 2008.

Yamamori, Tetsuanao, and Kenneth A. Eldred, eds. *On Kingdom Business: Transforming Missions through Entrepreneurial Strategies*. Wheaton, IL: Crossway, 2003.

Yoder, John Howard. *The Politics of Jesus*. Grand Rapids, MI: Eerdmans, 1994.

# VITA

Dru Alan Dodson
Birthdate: July 3, 1955, Little Rock, Arkansas
Contact Information: drudodson@gmail.com
Education:

> B.S. Mechanical Engineering, 1977. University of Arkansas, Fayetteville, Arkansas.

> M.A. Christian Thought, summa cum laude, 1992. Trinity Evangelical Divinity School, Deerfield, Illinois. The thesis *Philip Schaff, Princeton and the Idea of Church History* won the prize for best thesis in Christian Thought. Teaching Assistant for Dr. John Woodbridge.

> M.Div., summa cum laude, 1993. Trinity Evangelical Divinity School, Deerfield, Illinois.

> D. Min. Global Church-Based Theological Education, 2013. Gordon-Conwell Theological Seminary, South Hamilton, Massachusetts.

Professional History:

> Journeyman missionary with the Southern Baptist Convention, Jerusalem, Israel, 1977–1979

> Consulting engineer for various Arkansas, Tennessee, and Illinois firms, and owner of three start-up businesses, 1979–1992

> Steering committee and elder for the church plant Fellowship North, North Little Rock, Arkansas, 1983–1987

Planting pastor and teaching pastor, Lake Valley Community Church, Hot Springs, Arkansas, 1993–present

Started and owns, with wife Jo Helen, the restaurant Zoes, Hot Springs, Arkansas, 2007 – present

Director of Integrated Ministries, Go2 Network, Telford, Pennsylvania, 2011–present.

# THE GO2 NETWORK

We cultivate, resource and equip apostolic teams to establish kingdom initiatives and Kingdom Outposts in North America's multicultural areas (Ephesians 4:11–16).

- *The Calling of All Vocations to Mission:* GO2 believes that all Christian believers are priests before God, and that they participate in the program of God's mission through their work and vocations. Therefore, GO2 works with all believers, and not simply with clergy.

- *The Value of the Apostolic Team in Mission:* GO2 believes the apostolic team commissioned by the local church should be at the heart of the mission enterprise, actively engaged in it, and focused on mission as the key component that moves all ministry forward.

- *The Indispensable Fivefold Gifts for Mission:* GO2 believes that a singular focus on the pastor/teacher role in church planting shortchanges the mission of God. Ephesians 4:11–16 suggests at least five kinds of people given by Christ for apostolic team formation and mission expansion. These people include men and women from ALL vocations.

- *Partnerships:* GO2 seeks out and develops strategic partnerships in order to accomplish together what cannot be accomplished apart.

- *Expansion of the Gospel and the Kingdom:* GO2 believes the message and mission of the gospel is to expand to all peoples. This expansion reflects the growing influence of the kingdom of God on earth and so requires the holistic ministry of a community where the ethics of the kingdom are incarnated—a Kingdom Outpost.

- *Dependency in Prayer and the Stewardship of Gifts:* GO2 believes that only God's Holy Spirit has the capability to achieve His purposes in mission. We are chosen in Christ and sealed in the Spirit to join Him in His mission. Prayer is the ultimate sign of dependency and the use of spiritual gifting through a strong work ethic is the sign of stewardship. GO2 believes these two form the continuum upon which all mission and ministry rests.

More at www.Go2Ministries.com. The Go2 Network, 320 North 3rd Street, Telford, PA 18969. 877-222-2048 toll free.

Find more on *Kingdom Outposts*, the ideas, the team and the book, at www.KingdomOutposts.com.

Both a 6 minute trailer and a 20 minute film on the HaitiCure Project have been produced by GlobalStory2Film (www.globalstory2film.com). See the trailer at www.KingdomOutposts.com and find more information on receiving the full length film.

31601603R00165

Made in the USA
Lexington, KY
18 April 2014